Christian Orthodox
Political Philosophy

Christian Orthodox Political Philosophy

—— A Theological Approach ——

Pavlos M. Kyprianou

HOLY TRINITY PUBLICATIONS
Holy Trinity Seminary Press
Holy Trinity Monastery
Jordanville, New York
2023

Printed with the blessing of His Grace,
Bishop Luke of Syracuse and
Abbot of Holy Trinity Monastery

Christian Orthodox Political Philosophy: A Theological Approach
© 2023 Pavlos M. Kyprianou

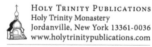

An imprint of

HOLY TRINITY PUBLICATIONS
Holy Trinity Monastery
Jordanville, New York 13361-0036
www.holytrinitypublications.com

ISBN: 978-1-942699-49-1 (paperback)
ISBN: 978-1-942699-53-8 (ePub)

Library of Congress Control Number: 2023933473

Cover Photo: "Stone relief, double-headed eagle"
Source: shutterstock.com / ID 1015110712 / © hakiagena

Contents

Foreword

During the Lord's questioning by the Roman Governor Pontius Pilate, the Saviour tells him: "My kingdom is not of this world" (John 18:36). This other-worldly origin is fundamental to an Orthodox understanding of the Church and inevitably raises questions as to how we should live in this present age and relate to those whom we live among. The ancient Greek philosopher Aristotle wrote that "Man is a political animal" and taught that as humans we cannot live in complete isolation from one another and so require some kind of structure to regulate our interactions with each other and our use of common resources. Political philosophy exists to inform what common structures and human interactions best serve the common good.

The Church understands that political action will not in itself bring us to salvation: "O put not your trust in princes, in the sons of men, in whom there is no salvation" (Ps 145:3). Nevertheless, the Church does interact with wider human society and for this reason it requires a political philosophy to guide its missionary course. This work seeks to elucidate the understanding of God and the Church that must ground an Orthodox political philosophy and offers concrete proposals of a contemporary nature as to how these ideas might be outworked. We may not always agree with these proposals in all their aspects but nonetheless hope that they will stimulate further prayer and discussion regarding alternative ideas.

It is our prayer that this work will be of an aid to the mission of the Church to sanctify all of creation and to avoid secularization while engaging with the world.

—Holy Trinity Monastery

Preface

I am fully aware that this is a difficult and elusive subject because it is widely believed that the Church is not (or should not) be involved in politics. I do, however, believe that Orthodox Theology has a contribution to make in the field of politics as well, since politics are typically a social art and science, and since Orthodox Theology teaches us that God Himself is a perfect society, or rather communion, of persons: of the Father, the Son, and the Holy Spirit.

A general source of inspiration for the work, without this implying full agreement regarding all the proposals contained within it, were the many homilies of my Elder, Metropolitan Athanasios of Limassol, which I was fortunate enough to start attending long before my tonsure as a monk in 2018, and which generally introduced me to the vast and beautiful world of theology, both theoretically and in terms of practical application in everyday life.

Professor Anestis Keselopoulos also gave me special inspiration and guidance regarding the present work, especially regarding the distinction between worldly secularization of the Church and churchly sanctification of the world, which I consider to be fundamentally important both for the present study and, generally, for the distinction, demarcation, and evaluation of Church activity within the world. His contribution was also crucial in reviewing and adapting some of the proposals set out in the original manuscript, through a fruitful and constructive discussion, and also in correcting some mistakes in the syntax and spelling of the original text which was written in Greek.

With this work, I would like to present in detail specific proposals inspired by Christian Orthodox Theology, concerning national and international politics, as well as Inter-Orthodox international relations, so that, through these proposals, I can contribute, with the help of God, to the development of a structured and integrated Christian Orthodox political thought.

The translation of this work from Greek to English was carried out by the author himself.

Pavlos M. Kyprianou (Monk Leontios)

Introduction

The Inspiration behind This Book

The inspiration behind this book was primarily the following observation[1]: on the one hand, the psychological dependence of a large portion of my Cypriot compatriots on ideologies with which they, intentionally or unintentionally, identify in a way that restricts their freedom of thought, and, on the other, the inclination of a large portion of the Church of Cyprus clergy to the right-wing "national(ist)" ideology, a fact which, at least at first sight, creates the impression and danger of the Church conforming with a secular pattern of this world, as is the case with any ideology.[2] Such a conformation with ideology may indeed cause or signify an infection within the spiritual hospital called the Church (regarding its human dimension), thus hindering her in her therapeutic work, especially concerning the liberation of the faithful from the disease of servile attachment and psychological dependence on ideology, given that the Church may itself be infected with the same disease.

An additional source of inspiration was, to some extent, the narration of an incident by a novice monk. He told me that, while attending the Theological Seminary in Nicosia in 2006, a suggestion had been made that a statue of Archbishop Makarios (for which a decision had been taken to remove it from the Archbishopric building) be placed in the precinct of the Theological Seminary. A large portion of the future clergymen who were students there reacted negatively, and among them a smaller portion also responded in a way that reached the limits of vulgarity in expressing their opposition and aversion to the implementation of this decision: Apparently they held the opinion that the policies of the late Archbishop Makarios[3] did not accord with their political views, and probably felt that the whole idea offended their patriotic or nationalist feelings. Of course, it is not for the present study to analyze the chapter

"Makarios" in modern Cypriot and international history, but surely this attitude of the future clergymen gives rise to a reasonable suspicion of a general tendency of conformation by a significant portion of the Cypriot clergy with a nationalist ideology, and also to a suspicion that they may be finding difficulty in distinguishing between Christ and Barabbas ...

In this way, the Church (in terms of her purely human and not divine constitution) could be seen as not always acting therapeutically vis-à-vis the divisive way of thinking encouraged by ideological parties (for the purpose of uniting their followers behind party lines), but instead acting in an aggravating manner: i.e., the Church to some extent identifies or allows herself to be identified with a secular, worldly pattern such as the "national(ist)" ideology. Such an approach, at least prima facie, appears to contradict the words of Christ that "My kingdom is not of this world."[4] This phenomenon, to the degree and extent that it exists, can also be considered as secularization or "worldly conformation" in the sense of an unhealthy conformation of the faithful with finite patterns of the fallen present world (e.g., ideologies), something that offends the Church in terms of her divine substance and mission in the world.

Aims of the Book

In light of the above thoughts, the aim of this book is to explore the borders and to propose criteria for distinguishing these boundaries between, on the one hand, a healthy adaptation of the Church with the world in order to facilitate her redemptive mission, and, on the other, an unhealthy "secularization," which conforms the Church to the world, thus weakening her redemptive power. The aim is also to apply these criteria and to propose a political philosophy, policy guidelines, and approaches on real issues which are, objectively, of crucial and current importance and relevance, concerning modern national and international politics, as well as Inter-Orthodox relations. In particular, this book, through these proposals, will seek to address issues concerning the best approach to be followed by the Church regarding:

a) The nation, the state, and the relationship between nation and state, and with the wider world.

b) Parties and ideologies.

c) The status of Russia as the most powerful Orthodox-majority state, and the possible implications of this power in terms of the Orthodox ecclesiastical hierarchy, as well as in terms of how decisions are reached by the ecumenical (universal) Orthodox Church on critical issues.

d) The issue of the Orthodox Diaspora and the best way to heal divisions within it, so that the missionary role of the Church can be conducted as effectively as possible.

This book aims to propose an Orthodox Political Philosophy on a number of critical and current political issues. These proposals derive legitimacy from Dogmatic Theology, the New Testament, Ecclesiastical History, and Canon Law. The Orthodox Political Philosophy that this book advocates is inspired by the ontology both of God as a loving communion of Persons, and of the characteristic of the Church as a single body with many members (see 1 Cor 12:12). That is why the proposed Orthodox Political Philosophy will seek to be person-centered and commune-centered, on both a local and an ecumenical scale.

Outline of the Book

The book will begin with an analysis of the ontological relationship between the Church and the world before the fall, how since then this relationship has disintegrated, and what are the implications of this dissolution regarding the role and mission of the Church in the world.

Next, the book will deal with the relationship between the Church and the nation, and will analyze, *inter alia*, the delicate balance that the Church must maintain in terms of the connection or association, but not identification, with the nation. This connection may facilitate the Church in her universal mission. But identification will secularize her. Furthermore, the concept of national self-transcendence for the sake of the union of nations in Christ from an ecumenical perspective will also be analyzed.

Then the relationship between Church and State in the light of the Gospel will be considered, in order to determine the correct boundaries of the legitimate confluence of Church and State so that, on the one hand, there is a maximum possible nonsecular adaptation of the Church to the world, but, on the other, conformation and secularization within the world are clearly and decisively avoided. Issues such as political systems, parties and ideologies, human rights, and economic policy will also be analyzed on the basis of theological criteria to the extent that this is realistically possible and within the understanding that the Church is in the world but, at the same time, not of this world.

An attempt will also be made to introduce proposals for the correction of distortions which are evident in the Orthodox Diaspora, in such a way that the irregularity of the presence of many (instead of only one) extraterritorial local Churches in one non-Orthodox majority country (e.g., U.K, France) is gradually corrected and at the same time positively utilized within the framework of missionary action in order to achieve the baptism into Orthodoxy of non-Orthodox nations.

Then there will be an attempt to synthesize and combine national and ecumenical consciousness using as a guiding principle the cohabitation of the local and ecumenical Orthodox Church. The purpose of the synthesis is to uphold the ecumenical character of the Church *via* (not bypassing) her local character, so that the universality of the Church is not an abstract, imagination-based (and thus baseless) ideology but a tangible reality and a standing invitation to non-Orthodox peoples to partake in it.

Finally, an attempt will be made to offer some proposals for correcting distortions and divisions that exist internationally in relations between, on the one hand, Orthodox-majority states belonging to the Western sphere of influence and, on the other, Russia, which is by far the strongest Orthodox-majority country and the freest from Western and potentially anti-Orthodox political influence. The main points of the proposals are the resolution of the problem of diarchy between the Greek and Russian world within Orthodoxy, the prospect of a federation or confederation of Orthodox-majority states without excluding non-Orthodox peoples, and the recognition of the Russian state as the "Geopolitical Protector of Orthodoxy."

Church and World

Brief History of the Church

Just as Christ is a real, historical person, so the Church, which Christ founded, has a historical existence. After all, theology without a historical context is not theology but mythology. We therefore consider it appropriate to quote, at the beginning of this chapter, a very brief, concise history of the One, Holy, Catholic and Apostolic Church,[5] with emphasis on her administrative structure:

"In the first millennium, with the religious freedom recognized by the edict of Milan [issued by the Emperor of the Roman Empire, Constantine, in 313 AD thus ending the persecutions against the Church, which was until then considered an illegal organization], five main ecclesiastical centers were formed: Rome, Constantinople (or New Rome), Alexandria, Antioch and Jerusalem. With the development of Christianity, various problems arose in the local Churches: threats from various sects, political intrigue, divisive tendencies and so on. The Synods of Orthodox Bishops were convened to deal with them. Some were local, while for the most serious issues, especially the dogmatic ones, the Ecumenical ones were held. The Ecumenical Council was convened by the Emperor but was always chaired by a Patriarch. In this way, the seven Ecumenical Councils of the indivisible Church of the first millennium were held. At the beginning of the second millennium, the painful ordeal of the Schism of the Churches between West and East took place (1054). A sad fact, which caused conflicts and obstacles in the spread of Christianity. Thus two administrative poles were created: In the West Rome, where in the middle of the [fourteenth and] fifteenth century protestant

1

movements appeared.[6] As a result, the gradual fragmentation of Western Christianity occurred as well as the creation of many ecclesiastical bodies. In the East, the four ancient patriarchates remained united, centered in Constantinople—New Rome, Alexandria, Antioch and Jerusalem. Great trials and tribulations followed after the Islamic invasions and conquests. At the same time, however, at the end of the first millennium, Orthodoxy developed significantly to the north with the Christianization of the Slavs and then the Russians. The Russian people as a whole came to the Orthodox faith and the Church continued her missionary effort of Byzantium in Northeast Asia. Thus a new ecclesiastical center was formed: the Moscow Patriarchate. From the middle of the fifteenth century until about the middle of the nineteenth, the Orthodox peoples of the Balkans, Asia Minor, the Middle East and North Africa lived under the Ottoman Empire. After the gradual liberation of the Balkan countries, the Ecumenical Patriarchate of Constantinople recognized [albeit not immediately] as Autocephalous the Churches of Greece, Serbia, Romania and Bulgaria. In the twentieth century, autocephaly was granted to the Churches of Poland, Albania, the Czech Republic and Slovakia, and the Churches of Bulgaria and Georgia were recognized as Patriarchates. The Church of Cyprus is Autocephalous by decision of the third Ecumenical Synod (fifth century)."[7]

The Church Is the Pre-fall World

The above description of the history of the Church focuses on the AD period. But in its own self-awareness, the Church constitutes the whole universal world and creation, both before and after the incarnation of Christ. The Church preceded Pentecost and the incarnation of the Divine Word. She existed before the creation of angels and humans. That is why the apostle Paul, drawing a comparison between Church and marriage, states the following: "Husbands, love your wives, just as Christ also loved the church and gave himself for her, that He might sanctify and cleanse her, … by the word, that He might present her to Himself a glorious church, not having spot or wrinkle or any such thing, but that she should be holy and without blemish."[8] Thus, Christ sacrificed himself for the Church (which existed before its "official" foundation on the day of Pentecost, and even before his incarnation) as well as for the whole created world, since the created world was in need of salvation as it had been dragged into corruption, and is still in corruption,[9] because of the original sin of man.[10]

From the inextricable and ontological relationship between the Church and the created world we see that the Church is by nature universal, but also the ark of salvation in the fallen world characterized by the disruption of divine harmony and order, which came about due to the original sin of man. After the fall, the Church is a microcosm of the universe and her mission is to transform the whole world into what it was before the fall, radiating in divine glory. Thus, the world must become Church again, and not the Church become world.[11] The ark must have its doors open for those who want to enter. There should be no exclusivity or exclusion, as it is the only way of salvation, and as the mission of the Church is to "make disciples of all nations, baptizing them in the name of the Father and of the Son and of the Holy Spirit."[12]

The Fallen World Is the Same as the Pre-fall World Only Now under Demonic Influence

The disobedience of the first-created, Adam and Eve, brought about the fall, an event that subjected the world to the law of corruption and placed it under demonic influence. The disobedience to God's commandment not to eat from the forbidden fruit was not an insignificant mistake but a disruption of man's relationship with God. The breakdown of the relationship was not an unintentional mistake but a voluntary choice of man in favor of self-deification. Man was deceived by the devil but he deliberately erred in a way that demonstrated his delusion in that he intended to become God without God. To become autonomous and self-sufficient. To become (contrary to nature) an individual isolated from God and not (through nature) a person who derives existence from his relationship with God (and his neighbor). The fallacy, of course, is that it is impossible for man to become God without God.[13] By choosing self-deification, man turned away from true deification, turned away from

God, who is the source of life itself, and thus inevitably subjected himself to death. Adam did not submit to the devil (like Judas in his decision to betray Christ[14]) but showed his preference for deification through individual knowledge (by eating from the tree of knowledge of good and evil) rather than through his loving relationship and communion with God. He preferred autonomy from God, in his delusion that it would lead him to self-deification. On the contrary, the act of "autonomization" led Adam and Eve to death, since they cut themselves off from the source of life, as God had predicted would happen and had warned them accordingly. He had warned them but did not stop them, because a coercive communion with God is not true communion. Communion presupposes love and love presupposes freedom.

But why did Adam's act of "autonomization" drag the whole human race in the same abysmal direction? Because he is our forefather, and through him the sin of attraction toward self-deification entered the body of the whole human race.[15] Because humanity is one single body with many members.[16] That is why the redemption of humanity necessitated the coming of the new Adam, Christ, as the new head of the body of humanity[17] who, as a God-man, has a relationship with God of a different nature than that between Adam and God, i.e., it is not a relationship of creator and created, but an ontological relationship of "being of one substance with the Father,"[18] and at the same time being 100 percent human (as well as 100 percent God).

In the meantime, the law was deemed necessary, i.e., the Mosaic Law, as a preliminary measure to deal with Adam's act of "autonomization," and to prepare the ground, as "our guardian to lead us to Christ,"[19] i.e., the new Adam. Through the law, man can realize his sinfulness[20] and ask, in repentance, for forgiveness and grace from God, which is "overabundant," in neutralizing the "increase in sin."[21] The law alone does not save, but rather faith that attracts the grace of God.[22] The law is important for us to realize our sinfulness and ask for forgiveness, but not to provide us with a *de jure* salvation by obeying its commandments. We keep the law not to be justified "by works of the law"[23] but to attract the grace of God. The obsession of most of the Jews with the priority of the law and its misinterpretation as an end in itself is another attempt at "autonomization" in deluded self-righteousness. A lost golden opportunity given (and still offered) by God for the use of the law in the direction of attaining communion with Him and achieving deification. It is a repetition of the fall at the moment when God gave and still offers to man the opportunity not only for healing the trauma of the fall but for utilizing it advantageously toward attaining deification, an option and feat which was not available to humanity, to the same degree, before the fall. This second fall of the Jews (in rejecting Christ) resulted paradoxically in the "reconciliation of the nations,"[24] but it will also eventually have the consequence of the return of Israel.[25] This second fall led and culminated in the crucifixion of the God-man Christ who humbly took death upon Himself and transformed it into Resurrection and Life in order to "destroy him who had the power of death, that is, the devil."[26] By the sacrificial crucifixion of Christ, God showed His absolute love, in such a manifest way that no one would hesitate to ask for God's mercy and grace, and in this way achieve his salvation.

For this reason, prostitutes and tax collectors "precede"[27] toward the kingdom of God, because they understand better (those who repent) that they are not saved by the law which they blatantly violated, but by the mercy and grace of God which they plead for persistently. The key to salvation is the tax collector's repentance and not the Pharisee's moral self-righteous, individualistic, anti-communal entrenchment within his ego. Repentance has the supra-rational, mysterious power to turn the fall into a blessing. The effects of the fall are not eliminated; they are transformed. The death that came from the fall remains a bitter cup, only now it has healing powers leading to eternal joy. The fall is and remains a fall but at the same time it is, in a mysterious and divine way, a blessing if man utilizes it properly.

Unfortunately, this was something that most Jews did not do. Their obsession with the Mosaic Law led to the rejection of Christ and ultimately to accursed deicide. The law came from God, but in the end most of the Jews preferred the law of God instead of God Himself! They preferred to resist communion with God using God's own law as a pretext.

It is as if they were saying to God: "Your law is enough for us, you stay away. Who told you that we want communion with you?" And of course, with their obstinate attachment to the law, they actually blatantly violated it and rendered it useless, as their (compatriot) Deacon Stephen pointed out to the fanatical group of Jews just before his stoning to death.[28] The fall of the Jews (i.e., those who did not follow Christ) is an example to be avoided but also a warning sign for Christians regarding the need for struggle against anti-communal "autonomization" from God, against self-righteous individualism, against the desire for self-deification.

The Relationship between the Church and the World after the Fall

Unfortunately, the fall of Adam and Eve was a triumph of the devil, as a result of which, he became the "ruler of the world" or "god of this age" even though his "victory" and defeat of the human race will eventually lead, according to the plan of divine providence, to the triumph of the Church and her elect. There are many who will not be saved because of their own indifference or aversion to God's love. For "many are called, but few are chosen."[29] The power of the devil after his diabolical "success" of bringing about the fall, will "force" the Church, based on the plan of divine providence, to be "in the world but not of this world" since "My kingdom is not of this [fallen] world."[30]

After the fall of Adam and Eve, the Church (before Christ) is pre-served in the persons of the Patriarchs and the righteous of the Old Testament, who have reached the vision of God,[31] and are preparing the way for the coming of the Saviour.[32] With the coming of Christ, the Church has become a perfect spiritual hospital,[33] with the ability to heal the wound in the common body of mankind that occurred due to the fall. To heal the attraction of mankind toward autonomy from God and self-deification, (which can manifest itself in various forms and variations), whether religious (through Pharisaic narcissism), or carnal (by elevating carnal pleasure to an object of worship), or ideological (with the elevation of an ideology to a supreme and absolute "truth" and object of worship). In all three cases idolization occurs and, through it, an inward tendency toward egoistic entrenchment, and a decomposition and masking of the person in a way which hinders or devalues communion with God and neighbor, since the masked individualist feels possessed of a false self-sufficiency that deludes him in bypassing communion with God and fellow man.

With His coming, Christ revealed the Church as a spiritual hospital able not only to heal the spiritually infirm, but also to resurrect the spiritually dead,[34] with the victory of God over death being celebrated daily through her sacraments in remembrance of Christ's sacrifice on the cross out of overwhelming[35] love for mankind and its salvation. Through these sacraments, and especially through the sacrament of Holy Communion, man is invited to repent and partake in spiritual healing, through loving communion with God and neighbor, which is the very essence of spiritual life in Christ.[36]

Therefore, the purpose of the Church is not to offer a new false self-sufficiency from God and fellow-man equivalent to the fall but through Church teaching and tradition, to inspire love for God and neighbor, since love is the fulfillment of the law,[37] leading, as evidenced by the Church's innumerable saints throughout the ages, to holiness and deification, i.e., perfect communion with Christ, the God-man, and with one another through Him.[38]

Churchly Sanctification of the World vs Worldly Secularization of the Church

The Church, due to the devilish "success" which brought about the fall, is "forced" to be in the world but not of the world (because the world is fallen). A crucial and decisive question regarding the relationship and activity of the Church in the world is the following: Is the "secular work" that she intends to carry out for the world serve the purpose of salvation of the world? Or does it distract from salvation and reduce the Church to a secular, charitable institution, a body in pursuit of upholding moral principles with the sole purpose to serve the smooth and proper functioning of society? If it serves the work of salvation, even indirectly, then the Church may express an opinion, she may manifest her presence, she may take a stand, she may act.[39] In the fallen world the Church is on "wartime" alert. She is fighting for the salvation of humanity. She does not have the luxury of looking down on and not employing means at her disposal, which may arise in the form of opportunities for utilizing institutions of the world (the state, for example) if these means are not sinful. It can, therefore, be said: the aim justifies the means; provided that the means are not sinful.

On the other hand, for the Church to be able to carry out her therapeutic mission, she must keep herself clean from the disease of worldliness. If she identifies (or conforms) with worldly patterns, she will inevitably become infected, and so she will not be able to function and execute her therapeutic role properly.[40] This is probably the biggest temptation the Church faces.[41] On the other hand, of course, she must be in the world and approachable, in order to be a perfect hospital in practice and not only in theory. So, the purpose of the Church is to make the world a Church as it was before the fall, and not the Church to become fallen world. That is why Christians should be in the world and at the same time not of the world.

Any conformation or identification with secular forms on the part of the Church will secularize her, reducing her to one, among many, secular institutions. On the other hand, the adaptation of the Church to local and contemporary political and social trends and patterns, and utilizing them within a framework of love and service, can help her carry out her mission of salvation more effectively, and fulfill her mission to "make disciples of all the nations,"[42] since the Gospel is a way of communal and social life and not an impersonal ideology within the sphere of either imagination or ideology or private, individualistic life.

On the one hand, therefore, conformation leads to a worldly secularization of the Church, while, on the other hand, adaptation promotes a churchly sanctification of the world. Secularization essentially means a self-negation of the Church, while sanctification refers to her revelation to the world, so that people can see her good works.[43] By aiming to sanctify the world, the Church expresses the reality that the battle for eternal life is given in this life and there will be no other opportunity. "Sanctification of the world" is thus consistent with, and is inspired by, the example of the incarnation of God the Word, by the incarnation of Christ and His full assumption of human nature without compromising in any degree his divine nature.[44] In this sense, the "sanctification of the world" by the Church, of the body headed by Christ, is necessary for our salvation, and any absence on her part will leave a spiritual void, which may be filled by Satan.[45] This incarnation of the Word of God, in a specific historical era and geographical area, also shows us that "sanctification of the world" has a personal, social, historical, local, loving, sacrificial dimension. It is *through* this "sanctification" that man will reach the (beyond time and place) heavenly paradise, and not by bypassing it. In other words, "sanctification" does not have an abstract, individualistic, ideological, utopian, impersonal character based on idols, ideas, or ideologies, which, as will be analyzed in the following chapters, are the antithesis of the Orthodox person-centered philosophy.

Secularization is the submission of the Church to the fallen world of demonic influence, and submission to the temptations of the devil. If Christ had succumbed to one of the devil's three temptations, we would not have a Church today but a triumph of the fallen world, a triumph of the devil. The devil essentially tempts Christ to submit to the fallen world, to triumph in a worldly manner, to turn stones into bread, to rule over the earth, and to perform miracles that leave no room for humanity to enter into a loving relationship with his Creator. The devil's proposal to Christ is essentially to *force* humanity to accept Him (Christ),[46] in a worldly rather than evangelical way. In this way there can be no real communion with Christ but a theocratic type[47] of slavish submission to Him. And of course, without communion with the God-man there is no deification and there is no immortality. There is only a conformation with the fallen world that cannot save us from corruption. Without communion with the source of life, that is Christ, we are inevitably subject to corruption and death.

Hence, secularization can be seen as a rejection or as a manifestation of indifference to the pursuit of a loving relationship and communion with Christ. This can happen not only by embracing another religion or even atheism, but also by moralizing, ideologizing, marginalizing, or even "depersonalizing" Christ, subjecting and subordinating Him to ideological or moral patterns or systems. It may also occur through a fundamentally flawed attempt to combine, on the one hand, faith, and, on the other, our service and submission to the passions and especially to the "giant" passions of lust, avarice, and ambition;[48] through our refusal to be crucified with Christ, and be resurrected with Him;[49] through our explicit or implicit agreement with those who mocked Him: "Let Him now come down from the cross, and we will believe Him."[50]

Secularization also means forgetting about the "city that is to come,"[51] i.e., forgetting our eternal and immortal existence, denying and forgetting that there is a God, whereas "sanctification" means that we have our attention turned to the "city to come," we know that it exists and we hope to become its citizens, and we are inspired by it in terms of our life and conduct in the transient city of our fleeting life. On the one hand, the transient city has a (short) expiration date, but on the other hand, it offers the unique opportunity and the entrance ticket for the future eternal life. We give exams in the transient city before moving on to the future one, and we pass these tests by following Christ's example of love and self-sacrifice to make the fleeting life as heavenly as possible in Christ, that is, as similar as it can be to the city to come. But we struggle knowing full well that our purpose is not to replace the "city to come" but to prepare ourselves for it. To prepare ourselves for perfect and eternal communion with Christ.

It is in essence an attempt to enter the city to come while we are still in the present city. An effort based on the teaching of Christ: "The kingdom of God is within [us],"[52] as well as that of Paul: "It is no longer I who live, but Christ lives in me."[53] In other words, the experience of the future eternal life begins within the present transient one. Not as an individualistic-subjective experience, but as a communal event, as a communal endeavor, which may take, generally speaking, two forms: in the form of an isolated, monastic life in the desert rather than in the city (because praying for humanity in a monastery or even in a cave in the desert is also a communal and not an individualistic endeavor), or in the form of living (as spiritually as possible) in the secular world. Either way, the education of the citizen for the city to come begins from the present transient city (or desert), so that we do not prove to be unfit second-class citizens in the "the city to come," the eternal kingdom of God.

In conclusion, "sanctification" refers to a struggle to see the Church being triumphant from the present transient life even if we know full well that this will be accomplished in its full glory after the Second Coming of Christ, i.e., within the eternal kingdom of God.

Church and Nation

The Nation as a Post-fall Phenomenon

The existence of nations[54] only became a reality in the post-fall world. There were no separate nations before the fall. The post-fall creation of nations can be traced to the Old Testament narrative of the Tower of Babel, where the people of that time were eager to build a tower that would reach to the sky in an attempt to surpass God and achieve self-deification. As a result of this arrogance, God, acting pedagogically, confused their languages so that the builders would not be able to communicate with each other, and so the grandiose work was thwarted. After this, mankind scattered throughout the earth: "Come, [they said,] let us build ourselves a city and a tower, whose top will reach to heaven; and let us make a name for ourselves, lest we be scattered abroad over the face of all the whole earth." But the Lord came down to see the city and the tower the sons of men built. Then the Lord said, "Indeed, the people are one race and one language, and have begun to do what they said. Now they will not fail to accomplish what they have undertaken. Come, let Us go down there and confuse their language, so they may not understand one another's speech." So the Lord scattered them abroad from there over the face of all the earth, and they ceased building the city and the tower. Therefore its name is called Babel, because there the Lord confused the languages of all the earth; and from there the Lord God scattered them abroad over the face of all the earth.[55]

Based on this narrative, the creation of peoples and nations can be considered to have been God's pedagogical reaction to man's selfishness and arrogance. Consequently, and by analogy, any union of nations and peoples would be beneficial only if it took place within a spirit of humility in Christ. It seems that the division of humanity into nations is intended to reduce the arrogance of the human race by putting a barrier to its self-destructive tendency toward self-deification. In this sense, and by extension, a multipolar world as an international system is the best option under these circumstances compared to the domination of a single superpower, especially if this superpower does not have as its main civilizational characteristic a political philosophy that is inspired or purports to be inspired by the "One Holy Catholic and Apostolic Church,"[56] which, from an Orthodox point of view, is none other than the Orthodox Church.

Nationalism as a Post-fall Ideology

If the creation of nations and races was the result of a fall (arrogance), then the elevation of the nation or race to a supreme idea, faith, or ideology (of ethnophyleticism or nationalism) constitutes a repetition or perpetuation of that fall. But before we move on, we must distinguish the terms "ethnophyletism" and "nationalism" from the term "patriotism." Ethnophyletism refers to an unwholesome love for the homeland, in a way which excludes love for the world as a whole, while patriotism means love both for the homeland and for the entire world. Genuine Christian love for the homeland does not reduce the love for the world but increases it, since the world is a magnificent creation of God. Christian love does not discriminate between nations since Christ gave His body and blood for all mankind. On the contrary, a distinction between the homeland and the world in a way that betokens hostility or indifference to the world is based on the ideology of nationalism which contradicts communion in Christ, since communion in Christ can never be hostile or indifferent, but instead is based on, and inspired by, absolute love.

The nationalist, in this sense, does not love the homeland as a specific place of communion, but as an impersonal idea and ideology. And, if the idol, idea, or ideology takes precedence over communion of persons, one can even harm the homeland herself for the sake of the ... idea of the homeland! Ethnophyletism is therefore an anti-communal version of the nation. It involves, so to speak, the division and partition of humanity not as an objective and inevitable description of a fact, i.e., the differences between nations and cultures that patently exist, but as a biased *prescrip*tion and confrontational projection of diversity as an end in itself. In other words, it is about dealing with differences between nations and cultures not just for the sake of well-meaning comparison, but for the sake of conflict. Ethnophyletism is not indicative of excessive love for the nation and the homeland, but rather an absence of love. Because genuine excessive love for the nation would overflow and spill over to the world at large.

Speaking of love, Christ clarifies that it should be directed (apart from God) to our "neighbor."[57] This is a clarification to certify the authentic, living, and communal nature of love. That is, love for either God, the nation, or the universe is authenticated by one's love for his neighbor, i.e., someone living in close proximity. In the absence of love for the neighbor, then any other love is unreal, unproven, or purely ideological (i.e., imagination-based and thus baseless). On the other hand, where there is love for one's neighbor and for God, according to Christ's commandment, a Christian perfection is attained that leaves no room for hatred toward any man or nation. Consequently, Christ's commandment to love one's neighbor, even if he is a foreigner,[58] and even if he is an enemy,[59] can create the foundation and framework of a communal and thus authentic (and not ideological-imaginary) patriotism and ecumenism in Christ.

Ideology as Division and Heresy

Since ethnophyletism is a divisive feature (as it confrontationally divides nations), if it is elevated to the sphere of theology, can it also be considered a heretical feature? In our opinion, yes, because ethnophyletism and hostility to foreigners may reach the point of idolatry, and also contradicts the teachings "make disciples of all the nations,"[60] "love one another,"[61] "love your enemies,"[62] and "love your neighbor as yourself,"[63] since the neighbor may be a foreigner, as seen in the parable of the Good Samaritan,[64] in the meeting of Christ with the Canaanite woman,[65] as well as in the discussion with the Samaritan woman.[66]

A classic example of ethnophyletism, without going into the underlying causes, or possible responsibilities for these causes that may have led to the occurrence of this event, was the establishment (by decision of the Ottoman authorities) of the Bulgarian Exarchate in 1870, within the jurisdictional boundaries of the Ecumenical Patriarchate of Constantinople, with a "flock" defined nationally and not locally. In other words, the Bulgarian Exarchate was created to attend to the spiritual needs of Bulgarians only, and within an area which belonged to the jurisdiction of the Ecumenical Patriarchate. This act was considered a schism and was condemned in 1872 at the Great Local Synod convened in Constantinople to address this issue. The Synod, which was attended by five prelates (Anthimos VI of Constantinople, Sophronius of Alexandria, Hierotheos of Antioch, Cyril of Jerusalem, and Sophronius of Cyprus) and two former Patriarchs of Constantinople (Gregory VI and Joachim II), condemned ethnophyletism as a sect, and as a teaching which is alien to the Orthodox faith. The decision of the Synod states, *inter alia*, the following:

"We renounce, censure and condemn phyletism, that is racial discrimination, ethnic feuds, hatreds and dissensions within the Church of Christ, as contrary to the teaching of the Gospel and the holy canons of our blessed fathers which support the holy Church and the entire Christian world, adorn it and lead it to divine [piety]."[67]

And a second example of ethnophyletism can be seen in the attitude of the Pharisees toward Christ. The "moral" basis for the Pharisees' betrayal of Christ to the Romans to be condemned to death was their concern that Christ's miraculous life and acts would endanger the Jewish nation in terms of their ethnophyletic identity, anticipating the feared reaction by the Romans to the continuation of Christ's mission.[68] These miraculous acts, instead of being considered a blessing and proof of Christ's divinity, were interpreted by the Pharisees as a threat to the nation or, rather, a threat to their position as representatives and leaders of the nation. In this way, the religious leadership of the Jews, even if their fears for their nation were genuine, which apparently were not—judging by their subsequent stance before Pilate[69]—placed the nation (and indirectly themselves as its leaders) above God, and showed that they were not so much interested in God as a divine person with whom they could lovingly commune, but only as an impersonal religious ideology, which, of course, they would continue to "defend," and from which they would continue to derive "guidance" and "identity" as "God's chosen people," to this day. In other words, they substituted faith in God as an impersonal idea or ideology or "law" for faith in God himself as a living, immortal person.

Sanctification and Self-transcendence of the Nation

Since the ideologicalization and idolization of the nation are a fall and a departure from the Orthodox spirit, the right approach should be the baptism and sanctification of the nation in Christ and in the Holy Spirit. The fact that the nation is a post-fall phenomenon does not mean that it is not open to sanctification and transformation through the Church. Thus, just as the family and marriage (which did not exist before the fall) can be sanctified, so can the nation. The nation, like marriage, must be integrated into an ecclesiastical and sanctifying context and direction, and be immersed in life-giving and sanctifying divine grace.

From a Christian point of view, the right attitude is to love our nation in response to Christ's commandment to love our neighbor. But we love our neighbor, because it is in our neighbor's person that love is authenticated in the sense of cohabitation with him, a feat that presupposes struggle and sacrifice. Whereas, on the other hand, the love for someone with whom we have no relationship or something to share, although it may reveal a positive predisposition, remains nonetheless somewhat unproven and effortless. Love for the homeland and the nation must be integrated within the context of spiritual struggle in Christ and His commandment to love; a love which excludes no one (neither the enemy[70] nor even the devil[71]) and is substantiated and "proven" in the form of cohabitation and forgiveness with one's neighbor.

Any separation and detachment of the love for one's nation from love in Christ carries the risk of reducing the nation into one of the many idols of this transient fallen world, idols which are isolated and immune from eternal life, and destined to perish along with those people who believe in them. Furthermore, in the absence of divine grace, the nation and nationalism can even reach levels of satanic idolatry, as seen in Nazism, where everything was allowed and justified, even genocide, for the sake of the nation and racial purity.[72]

The purpose of the Church is therefore the sanctification of both the world and of the nations, their rebirth in Christ. This does not mean the abolition of nations, but their sanctification may provide the impetus and inspiration for the transcendence of the nation to meet other nations in communion on the basis of Orthodox civilization. But, of course, since sanctification is a divine energy, the degree, extent, and quality of national self-transcendence for the purpose of uniting two or more nations cannot be fully predetermined as a general and absolute rule. It is a matter of discernment to what extent it is beneficial for one nation to approach and unite with another, even if they are united by the common Orthodox faith.

How does the Church contribute to the sanctification of the nation? Not by making the Church a national institution in conformation with secular patterns, but rather by inspiring the nation to a sacrificial and loving "emptying" of itself for the sake of the other people, but without submitting to their nationalism. This is because if they submit to the nationalism of the other nation, both will be harmed, since submission will not inspire the other nation to follow the sacrificial way of Christ, but will encourage it to follow an opposite oppressive, antichristian, and mutually damaging course of action.

But is there a geographical and local limitation to the commandment of love? We believe that Christ, by teaching us to love our "neighbor" specifically, shows that love has a personal and communal character, rather than individualistic, ideological, and abstract one. Love means giving, emptying, and sacrificing for the sake of the other, and this usually presupposes a common place and time where the meeting takes place.[73] On the other hand, if by his actions, and by his position, a person can influence either people in another geographical area or future generations, then surely the concept of place and time may expand as well as the concept of "neighbor." The fact that the extension of this term (spatially or chronologically) entails the use of human imagination is a fact that requires, as a necessary counterweight, due care so that this imagination is not elevated above, but subjected to, the communion of persons. This extension should aim at serving and not negating the communion of persons. And the safest way to authenticate, substantiate, and subject an idea to communion of love between persons is via sacrifice: i.e., sacrificing something of value in order to authenticate your love. In this way, there is a significant counterweight to ideologicization. It will guarantee that belief in the fraternity of nations is not just an ideology based on individual (impersonal) imagination, but a living experience authenticated by loving sacrifice.

We believe, in connection with the above, that Christ's commandment to His disciples to "make disciples of all the nations"[74] was certainly given in a loving and sacrificial context. Regarding the commandment to love one's neighbor, it was not intended to make a negative and exclusionary distinction between neighbor and non-neighbor, but a positive distinction: love your neighbor and through your neighbor love all humanity and God Himself. After all, while Christ lived in a specific geographical place and in a specific historical period, His acts and His sacrifice on the cross were for the benefit of all mankind. In fact, it was a sacrifice that, as He prophesied, would movingly inspire people from the East and West, and not those directly close to him (neighbors), as were His compatriots.[75] And of course the example of Christ is imitated by the holy apostles, as well as many other saints who are considered, from an ecclesiastical point of view, as teachers and luminaries of the whole world, and not just their compatriots.

The Mission of the Jewish Nation to the World

From a Christian as well as a Judaic point of view, the mission of the Jewish nation was to maintain the faith in the one true God, and to give birth to the Messiah, to be "a light to bring revelation to the Gentiles, and the glory to Your people Israel."[76] The fundamental difference is that from a Christian point of view, the Messiah has come, and He is Jesus Christ, while from a Jewish point of view the Messiah has not yet come, and when He does come, according to the Gospel and ecclesiastical awareness, He will be the Antichrist.[77] From a Christian point of view, then, the mission of the Jewish nation was to give birth to Christ in revelation and salvation of all nations, to accept Christ as the Saviour of the world, and then to naturally become "one flock"[78] along with other nations that would also accept Christ. But this would entail the loss of the special religious identity of the Jewish nation as the "chosen people of God," as they would no longer differ, from a religious point of view, in any respect compared to other peoples who would also accept Christ as the Saviour of the world. So the Jews had before them the great challenge and invitation to sacrifice their national-religious identity for the sake of the salvation of other nations (as well their own). To crucify their identity, their national ego, for the sake of humanity. Unfortunately, most Jews, led by their political-religious leaders, did not follow this sacrificial way.

It should be noted, however, that there was a significant portion of Jews who followed the Christian faith. They gradually ceased to have Jewish self-consciousness after their Christianization, and that is why today Judaism and Christianity are considered mutually exclusive identities. In other words, from a Christian point of view, these Jews achieved national self-transcendence to an admirable and exemplary extent, because of which they acquired a new religious identity which abolished and replaced their previous national-religious identity. The contribution of the Christians of Jewish origin in the consolidation and spread of Christianity, in its first critical steps, is indirectly referred to in Paul's letter to the Romans, where it is stated, *inter alia*, that the Christians of Macedonia helped the Christians of Jerusalem materially not only out of kindness but also out of obligation since Christians had benefited from the spiritual gifts of the Jewish Christians.[79] Indeed, among the Jews who accepted Christ as the Messiah were the so-called Hellenistic Jews, who were in fact the driving force for the spread of Christianity to other nations. The first references to the Hellenistic Jews, that is, the Jews of the diaspora, are found in the narration of Pentecost in the Acts of the Apostles, where we are informed that those witnessing and participating in the revelation of the Holy Spirit were Jews "dwelling in Jerusalem, devout men, from every nation under heaven."[80] So these are Jews of the diaspora who had a Hellenistic cultural background but without abandoning Judaic monotheism. Among the Hellenistic Jews were Paul, Barnabas, and Stephen. A clearer reference to the Hellenists is made by Luke in the Acts of the Apostles, stating that "in those days, when the number of the disciples was multiplying, there arose a complaint against the Hebrews by the Hellenists, because their widows were neglected in the daily distribution."[81] This verse "is very important because ... it speaks of the existence of two groups of Christians in the life of the ancient church, the 'Hellenists' and the 'Hebraics' and implies that there are some disagreements within the first Christian community ... [The Hellenists] had the Hellenistic language as their mother tongue and were obviously influenced by the Hellenistic spirit and the Hellenistic culture of the diaspora."[82]

Therefore, they had a more open and ecumenical spirit, which proved to be a catalyst for the spreading of Christianity. The final victory of ecumenical Christianity took place at the Synod of Jerusalem in 49 AD, where it was decided that to join the Church it was not necessary to first embrace Judaism and be circumcised, thus paving the way for Christianity to spread throughout the world.[83]

How Christ Viewed His Own Nation

Undoubtedly, Christ loved His nation. That is why with great pain and paternal (and divine) love He will proclaim: "O Jerusalem, Jerusalem, the one who kills the prophets and stones those who are sent to her! How often I wanted to gather your children together, as a hen gathers her chicks under her wings, but you were not willing!"[84]

He was a Jew with national consciousness and gave priority to the Jews in terms of their evangelization, as seen in His interaction with the Samaritan woman,[85] in His dialogue with the Canaanite woman,[86] and in directing His disciples to give priority to the lost sheep of the house of Israel.[87] This priority did not mean indifference or exclusion of other nations, as can be seen in the parable of the Good Samaritan, where the term "neighbor" refers to the foreign Samaritan.[88] The priority to His nation is not directed against the world, but for the benefit of world. It is not for the salvation of the nation instead of the world, but for the salvation of the former in order to achieve the salvation of the latter. This priority was one of duty of the Jewish nation and not a precedence of privilege. In many passages of the Gospel, the love of Christ for every person regardless of nationality is clearly seen through the miracles He performed for them, such as the healing of the centurion's servant,[89] of the daughter of the Samaritan woman,[90] and of the Samaritan leper,[91] and these acts were of course part of His mission to save the whole world. In fact, Christ prophesied the following: "I say to you that many will come from east and west, and sit down with Abraham, Isaac, and Jacob in the kingdom of heaven. But the sons of the kingdom will be cast out into outer darkness. There will be weeping and gnashing of teeth."[92] Christ warns as seen from the above and other passages, that the "inheritance" will be taken from the Jews and be given to the nations. For example: "What will the owner of the vineyard do to them? He will come and will destroy these vinedressers and will give the vineyard to others"[93] And also: "See, your house is left to you desolate."[94]

It should also be noted that Christ did not seem to believe in liberation struggles nor did He ever express a "great idea" of delivering the Jews from the Roman yoke. This clearly distinguishes Him from the rebel and murderer Barabbas, to whom the Jews in the end appear to have shown greater honor than to Christ.[95] The recognition, on Christ's part, of Roman power is evident, *inter alia*, in two passages: "Tell us, therefore, what do You think? Is it lawful to pay taxes to Caesar, or not?" But Jesus perceived their wickedness, and said ... "Render therefore to Caesar the things that are Caesar's, and to God the things that are God's."[96]

Regarding the Jews' preference for Barabbas instead of Christ (as expressed by the Jewish crowd assembled at the Praetorium courtyard and after so being persuaded by their leaders) a plausible explanation is that they preferred a nationalist who was engaged in violent struggle against the Romans with the aim of creating a Jewish kingdom which would dominate the world, rather than a leader who envisaged His own nation as an apostle and servant of nations in the context and prospect of the eternal kingdom of God. They showed their preference to a violent revolutionary to a spiritual revolutionary of love and self-sacrifice.

Thus, we can say that the betrayal of the Jewish nation generally (even if not of all its members) of Christ was the rejection of their own king on the grounds that He was not preaching a worldly redemption and domination over all nations, but of the need to sacrifice for them. The following passage is indicative of their betrayal: "They cried out, 'Away with Him, away with Him!, crucify Him!' Pilate said to them, 'Shall I crucify your King?' The chief priests answered, 'We have no king but Caesar!'"[97] The God-inspired (according to Orthodox Christianity) Bible presents the betrayal against Christ (in the absence of repentance) as a crime committed by the Jewish nation generally and perpetually through the generations to come, and not just by their chief priests and leaders: "And all the people answered and said, 'His blood be on us and on our children.'"[98]

It is also worth noting, however, that at some point after the miracle of the multiplication of the loaves and the fish, the Jews who witnessed the miracle decided to make Christ their king, and yet He refused. "When Jesus perceived that they were about to come and take Him by force to make Him king, He departed again to the mountain by Himself alone."[99] Why did he avoid the coronation? Because "My kingdom is not of this world."[100] So what are the political implications? Why was Christ not comfortable with acquiring worldly authority to assist Him in His spiritual work? How is this reconciled with the view that the Church should adjust to power structures so that it may carry out its redemptive mission more effectively? How indeed does this fit with Byzantium, the multinational empire with Orthodoxy at its core? We believe that the reason for Christ's rejection of the proposal to become an earthly king lies in the fact that the teaching of Christ is not a philosophy or ideology which he wanted to impose authoritatively. Rather, the essence of His teaching was love; love that leads Him willingly to crucifixion and to resurrection. Apparently these people wanted to invest Him with secular power and not just secular influence. In the former case there is an adverse effect on the freedom of the person, while, in the second, respect for the person's freedom is adequately safeguarded. Christ was not in favor of creating new authoritarian structures, but rather sanctified existing ones. He was and is a heavenly king and not an earthly one. He was and is a High Priest[101] and not an earthly king or emperor. He was not in favor of attaining power, but was and is appealing for universal participation, lords and subjects, wealthy and poor, to follow Him in the path leading to absolute love, manifested sacrificially through crucifixion and resurrection.[102]

The Fall out of Christ with the National Establishment

Christ did not shy away from confronting the Pharisees, that is, the religious and political leaders of the Jewish people. This is because the Pharisees were abusing their authority as advocates and interpreters of Mosaic Law with the aim of enhancing their dominant and privileged position over the Jewish people.[103] They were not ready to accept, as it became evident after the crucifixion of Christ and the first steps of the Church, the view that the Law was "our tutor to bring us to Christ."[104] They were not ready to accept the abolition of the Law for the sake of the creation of a new humanity, with Jews and Gentiles being brothers.[105] And this is obviously because they would lose their privileges as leaders of their nation. The ruler of the nation would be Christ who would not be a national but a world leader and at the same time a servant, that is, without institutionalized political power. The Jews would lose their exclusivity as the chosen people, a privilege that they wanted to use in their quest for power over the world rather than share it with the world. Thus we have the astonishing and paradoxical phenomenon of Christ, who was a Jew, being worshiped by the Gentiles and rejected by his compatriots[106] because of their inability to overcome the distinction between Jews and Gentiles, thus choosing to remain attached to their ethnophyletism and in their sense of national and cultural superiority.

The failure of the Jews to achieve national self-transcendence is not an occasion for triumphalism among the nations which accepted Christ, but a warning to them to avoid the same error, and an exhortation to walk the difficult path leading to crucifixion and resurrection, within the framework of a constant national self-transcendence, a continuing effort to remove national obstacles that either potentially or actually cause divisions within the one ecumenical flock.[107] Indeed, the spiritual fall of the Jews is an example to be avoided by the nations, so that their acceptance of Christ is not superficial and undermined by an indirect rejection of Him through the upholding of a "national" Christ, subordinating Him to a nationalist ideology. Such an approach would be a distortion of the Gospel because Christ is above everything, and supreme authority in heaven and on earth,[108] and therefore He is not subservient to the nation. On the contrary, the nation is under him, and should be constantly seeking to be spiritually enriched and sanctified by His divinity. The history of every Christian nation should begin, in its collective consciousness, from its Christianization, from its baptism, which means death and resurrection.[109] Death of the old man and resurrection of the new man reborn in Christ. Death of the old nation and resurrection of the new nation reborn in Christ.

How the Apostle Paul Viewed His Own Nation

Paul's love and pride for his nation are indisputable. His whole life, both before and after his baptism, testifies to this fact. It should be noted, however, that, like Christ himself, Paul did not show any interest in shaking off the Roman yoke and "liberating" his Jewish compatriots. On the contrary, he himself was a Roman citizen, an important privilege of the time, and he does not hesitate to make use of it when, for example, he risks being punished without trial.[110]

Paul initially focused his efforts on convincing his fellow Jews that Christ is the Messiah. When he was faced with their intransigence and unrepentance, Paul lost his patience and told them directly that they themselves bear responsibility for their spiritual loss, and that he would now concentrate his efforts on evangelizing the gentiles. He initially gave priority to the Jewish nation, but refused to identify himself with it, but instead followed an ecumenical direction, and was thus universally recognized by the Christian world as the "Apostle of the Nations." In other words, when he saw that his own nation refused to fulfill its ecumenical mission, he did not hesitate to proceed in his God-given ecumenical mission without his nation. The fact that his countrymen refused to comprehend this mission was certainly not sufficient reason to prevent Paul from undertaking and pursuing this mission to the nations. In any case, Paul's turn to the nations does not signify an abandonment of his nation, about which he even prophesies that they will eventually convert to Christ.[111]

Indicative of Paul's superiority and freedom in terms of his non-attachment to any nation (or with its narrow interests) are the following passages from the New Testament: "There is neither Jew nor Greek, there is neither slave nor free, there is neither male nor female; for you are all one in Christ Jesus."[112] Moreover: "For though I am free from all, I have made myself a servant to all, that I might win the more; and to the Jews I became as a Jew, that I might win the Jew; to those who are under the law, as under the law [though not being myself under the law] that I might win those who are under the law; to those who are without the law, as without the law (not being without law toward God, but under law toward Christ), that I might win those who are without the law; to the weak I became as weak, that I might win the weak. I have become all things to all men, that I might by all means save some. Now this I do for the gospel's sake, that I may be partaker of it with you."[113]

The National Self-transcendence of the Greek Nation for the Sake of a Christian World

Unlike the majority of Jews, the Greeks became and remain a Christian nation in that the overwhelming majority of its members identify as Christian Orthodox. By accepting the Christian faith, they inevitably turned their backs on their pagan past, because these two dimensions cannot coexist from a Christian point of view, since, for Christians, Christ is the only truth who can lead to salvation.[114] The rupture with the past was so deep that the term "Greek" was, for many centuries, a collective name for those Greeks who chose to remain attached to the pagan religion of their ancestors, while those who chose to become Christians preferred the name "Roman" derived from the Roman Empire (later and retrospectively called "Byzantium" by historians) with Constantinople—New Rome, as its capital. It could be said that the baptism of Hellenism in Christ was accompanied by a change of their national name.

Of course, the transfer of the capital of the Roman Empire from the West to the East was an important factor encouraging the aforementioned national transcendence, since this change was accompanied by the grad-ual dominance of the Greek language over Latin, and the acquisition by Greeks of high positions in various sectors of the empire. Thus, in a way, the Greeks agreed to become Romans, when the Roman Empire became, in a sense, Greek. But this reason alone is not enough to explain the change of the national name from Greeks to Romans. Because, if the only reason for the change of national name was the dominant position of the Greeks in the Roman Empire (with Constantinople as its capital), then why did they not prefer to rename the Roman Empire itself into "Greek Empire," but chose instead to rename themselves from Greeks to Romans and preserve the name of the state as "Roman Empire"?

Undoubtedly, the rejection of the name "Greek" as a national name was to an extent connected to the great political and cultural brilliance of the Roman Empire, which was the most powerful empire in the world for many centuries and, a Christian empire, with the Church generally enjoy-ing considerable political influence, and being a source of inspiration and a source of civilizational and spiritual identity for rulers as well as sub-jects.[115] In other words, the magnificence of the Christianized Roman state encouraged the Romans to abolish their former national name "Greek" and thus express their strong conviction that given that they have accepted Christ as God-man and Saviour, then, in a way, everything must change, even national consciousness and identity, in the sense that Christianity is not just a new religious investment placed on top of an existing national identity, but a new identity religiously, culturally, and nationally, reaching deep into the heart of the nation and bringing about its rebirth in Christ. By changing their national name, and giving priority to religious, cultural, and state identity over the ethnic one, the Romans appealed to the world for universal unity of nations on the basis of the common faith in Christ.[116]

With the rebirth of the Greek nation in Christ, the Greek language, as well as philosophy, was put to the service of the Gospel in order to express its meanings as accurately and deeply as possible, but also to dis-tinguish the Christian truth from delusion and heresy, precisely through the answers given by the Church to philosophically oriented views and questions.[117]

This is perhaps why the Church, encouraged by the new national Roman identity, had the power to speak out against the Ancient Greeks and their errors in her literature and sacred texts, wanting to emphasize the break with the past. Given the rupture of the Church Fathers with Greek national identity during the period of the Christianized Roman Empire, the Church today could encourage the reinstatement of "Roman" as a national name, perhaps not in replacement of the name "Greek," but as a complementary name.[118] Otherwise, inevitably, the Church will have to live with the following contradiction: on the one hand exalting *Greek* Orthodoxy, and on the other hand preserving in its sacred books a multitude of accusations against the *Greeks* and their delusions. One could answer: "But then the term 'Greek' was synonymous to 'pagan.'" It is indeed true that Greek meant pagan, but that is exactly because the Greeks *were* pagan. That is, paganism was a key feature of the Ancient Greek identity, so based on this fact there was a theological basis for anti-Hellenism in the Church's sacred texts. It was not, of course, anti-Hellenism based on racial grounds (since the authors of the texts themselves could have been Greeks or descendants of Greeks), but a cultural and religious anti-Hellenism. From the meaning that the Fathers gave to the term "Greek," it follows that it is very far-fetched to consider the acceptance of Christianity by the Greeks as a continuation and fulfillment of Ancient Greek civilization. Because if that were the case, then they would not have been speaking against Greek delusions in their sacred texts. We cannot consider that Greek culture was a "tutor to bring us to Christ,"[119] as was the case with the Jewish civilization. But this is not demeaning to the Greeks because, despite the fact that the Jews had a civilization that was a "tutor," the majority of them did not manage to creatively transcend their attachment to their national identity for the sake of the perfection and fulfillment of their civilization in Christ,[120] in contrast to the Greeks who proved, through their feat of national self-transcendence, the authenticity of their search for truth, in their humble acceptance of the superiority of Christianity to their great civilization. It would therefore be self-defeating for the Greeks if this national self-transcendence which is evident in the anti-Greek passages of the holy texts of the Fathers of the Church was simply attributed to a coincidental synonymy of the words "Greek" and "Pagan." Because the synonymy was not accidental but an intentional association, revealing the Christian fathers's intention to break with the national past and to emphasize the fact that, with their Christianization, the Greeks were reborn into a new nation, and consequently must have a new name. Adhering to this approach, the Fathers of the Church seem to have applied the words of Christ: "And no one puts new wine into old wineskins; or else the new wine bursts the wineskins, the wine is spilled, and the wineskins are ruined. But new wine must be put into new wineskins."[121]

This rupture of the Greeks with their own national identity, when paganism was a key characteristic of it, was an example of the prioritization of the Christian faith above the nation, resulting, not in its abolition, but rather rebirth in Christ. Now that paganism has ceased to be a characteristic of Hellenism, there is no longer the same need (from a Christian perspective) for anti-Hellenism, since the Greek nation is a Christian Orthodox nation. Be that as it may, the reemergence (from ancient times) of the national name "Greek" (after the creation of the modern Greek state in 1827) in replacement of "Roman," gives the impression of a lack of appreciation for the national self-transcendence achieved by the nation with its baptism for the sake of Christianity (some fifteen centuries before the creation of the modern Greek state).

Given the above, and that the Roman Empire with its capital in Constantinople—New Rome was a multinational state (albeit with a predominance of the Greek language), it can be concluded that the Church is not opposed to national self-transcendence when this promotes the fraternity of nations within a commonwealth of Orthodox states, or even within a common federal structure on the basis of a common Christian Orthodox civilization.[122] This national self-transcendence can be expressed by removing a national name for the sake of a common name acceptable to all participating nations. Should such an opportunity for the integration of Hellenism into a supranational, multinational, Christian Orthodox state arise, of which Greeks will be (among others) its citizens, then the state name should probably be given priority in terms of national consciousness over the national name "Greek." This is not tantamount to abolishing the narrow national identity, but to relegating it to second place for the sake of the overriding state-centered, multinational identity. Such a course of action should lead not to historical discontinuity but to national transcendence setting an example for other nations to follow. In this way, a new national consciousness is created, which we must also be ready to overcome if need arises for the sake of unity in Christ with other Christian Orthodox nations.[123]

But can this have consequences regarding the sense of historical continuity? Possibly yes. That is why any national transcendence should be a step forward and not backward; a step toward integration in Christ, and not toward national disintegration; a step toward state and national strengthening and not weakening. If, for example, the European Union was a union of Orthodox-majority states (or if it had a strong Orthodox core similar to that of the Russian Federation) then the Church could support national self-transcendence by supporting the case for elevating the name "European" over "Greek" in the national consciousness of the people. But since the abovementioned Orthodox precondition is not met, the Church cannot and should not give her blessing to such a change.

Christian Orthodoxy vis-à-vis National Power, Resistance, and Liberation

It is God's commandment to become servants if we want to become great.[124] To be servants deliberately and from a position of power (and not weakness). The most useful and reliable servant is the powerful servant.[125] Provided he uses his power humbly in the service of others. Thus, to serve the world, a nation must seek to become powerful, not to rule over others, but to serve humanity, and even its enemies,[126] with humility.

In order to protect the land and its people, the Church can give its blessing for armed resistance to invaders and, with especial discernment, to liberation struggles, on the basis of the principle "choose the lesser of two evils." The struggle must be for faith and motherland, and without abandoning one's love for the enemy. Armed struggle can be legitimate in Christ if it does not abolish love for the enemy. Of course, it must be a struggle with self-sacrifice until the bitter end. But without hatred. If hatred, which is a demonic energy, dominates our soul, then it is like playing a game with the devil as judge. We give him the right, in some way, to judge the conflict. We indirectly (and delusionally) invite the devil to help us win if the true God does not respond positively to our request to enable us to crush the hated enemy. That is why the correct prioritization is important, first faith (based on love) and then motherland. We must first arm ourselves with the weapons of love, and then with the weapons of war.

Although the line between defensive and offensive warfare may sometimes be very thin, nonetheless it can be stated that it is very difficult to combine a purely offensive and aggressive war with love for the enemy. Whereas in the case where war is defensive, and justice is clearly on our side, this strengthens us spiritually to have the power to love the enemy, even if we have to defeat him, since destroying him is a better option for him as well, as he is prevented from harming himself eternally by committing war crimes. Of course, Christ did not resist His enemies. However, at the scene of His arrest, He protected His disciples, telling the people who came to arrest Him: "I have told you that I am He. Therefore, if you are seek Me, then these go their way."[127] He would probably have resisted defensively and self-sacrificially had His enemies sought to crucify not Him but His disciples, calling upon the crucifiers to crucify Him and leave His disciples in peace. He would have sacrificed Himself for both His disciples and His enemies, as He in fact did. But how can we imitate this act in case of war? Sacrificing ourselves while fighting, or by remaining unarmed and passive? If we remain unarmed the enemies will easily neutralize an obstacle in their attempt to harm our compatriots. If we sacrifice ourselves in battle, we sacrifice ourselves for our compatriots who are "our neighbors" and at the same time we prevent the enemy from committing crimes against both our fellows and himself, given that if he commits the intended crimes he will damage his own soul before God eternally. But one could object: "Then why did not Christ prevent Judas from betraying Him and leading Him to crucifixion?" This could be answered as follows: He did not prevent Judas from carrying out this betrayal, because He respected his freedom and because He would be sacrificing Himself as a result of it, and not someone else. Furthermore, Christ had originally asked his Father to "allow" Him not to pass the great ordeal of submitting to the wickedness and betrayal of His fellow human beings. Of course, Christ obeyed his Father's will to fulfill His sacrificial mission on earth, but, on the other hand, we can never, and perhaps to do so would be a blasphemy, characterize Christ's original desire as a sinful example to be avoided. Hence, we believe that we are imitating Christ by sacrificing ourselves, following our conscience with simplicity and without legalism, asking for strength and enlightenment from God, and at the same time giving God the right to prevent us from actions that may not be pleasing to Him. So we believe that imitating the attitude of Christ is best achieved by trying to destroy an enemy who is unjustly attacking us, for the sake of our friends and neighbors, but also for the sake of the foes themselves. In this way we are complying with the spirit of sacrifice for the sake of friends and foes alike, avoiding the legalistic approach of Jehovah's Witnesses, who would refuse armed resistance to aggressors even if they were posing a severe threat to their family and neighbors.[128]

Conclusion: Cohabitation, Adoption, and Ecumenization of the Nation by the Church within the Church, and through the Church

In conclusion we can state that the purpose and mission of the Church in relation to the nation is to make it Orthodox. That is, to make it holy, saved, and sanctified in Christ from this life and reaching to eternity. Not necessarily by abolishing it, but by recreating it in Christ. To achieve this, the Church may:

a) Support and unite the nation but not identify with it, nor become subservient to it.[129] For if Orthodoxy becomes a national religion, then with what conviction and justification will an Orthodox nation endeavor to make disciples of other non-Orthodox nations, in accord with Christ's commandment, without this effort being motivated or appear to be motivated by ulterior nationalist motives? Such an approach would be characteristic of the behavior of certain Jewish Christians of early Church history, which Paul condemns: "As many as desire to make a good show-ing in the flesh, these would compel you to be circumcised ... that they may boast in your flesh."[130]

b) Not be detached from the nation, because the mother does not sepa-rate from her child unless the nation rejects her, and even then the Church (being a mother) does not renounce her motherhood.

c) Commune with the nation and at the same time help to bring this nation in communion with other nations, because the Church has a local and at the same time universal character, as she is the mother of many nations.

In conclusion, the Church should seek to cohabitate with the nation, to adopt the nation with its free consent, and to ecumenize the nation.

Church and State

The State as a Post-fall Phenomenon

In paradise there was no need for states and governments, since man was united in God by His grace and love, and had no knowledge of evil. Since he had no knowledge of evil, there was no need for law or policing to act as a deterrent to crime. Since he was immortal, there was no need for laws to prevent or warn of dangers to human safety and health. Since there was plenty of everything to meet the "needs" of man without the need for work, there was no reason for laws to regulate economic relations between people and classes of people. Since people were not divided into nations and languages, there was no international conflict, and no need for state organization to strengthen the position or defense of one state against another. Since people were immersed and felt fulfilled in their personal relationship with God, and since the world was perfect, they had no need for ideologies with which to identify, nor the need for state power to impose them on others. Perhaps for these reasons Christ stressed that His own kingdom is not of this world.[131] Nevertheless, despite the post-fallen origin of the state, there is no reason to believe that the state, like marriage, and like the nation,[132] is not receptive to sanctification.

The Recognition of the Role of the State by the Church

The state serves a noble purpose because it offers, or has the ability to offer, order and stability.[133] For the Church, the state should be considered as an edifice that offers protection and opportunities enabling her to carry out her own work within the spiritual sphere. The Church which "rejoices with those who rejoice,"[134] can enrich the love and respect between citizens and the state by giving it a superior beauty and an eternal perspective.

The State and the Church can coexist and cooperate for the benefit of the people, while both maintaining their independence. The Church may be strengthened by the persecution and blood of her martyrs, but she would never want to force anyone to become a martyr, nor would she favor or advocate the creation of conditions of chaos and persecution by the state in order to increase her martyrs.

Christ was a law-abiding citizen and did not oppose obedience to worldly authorities, if they did not violate God's law.[135] The same is true of the apostle Paul. At the same time, the state should facilitate obedience and respect for the law by the citizen, by also respecting the dignity of the citizen, without whose contribution the state cannot exist. In other words, just as children (the people) must submit to their parents, so parents (the state) must not "provoke children to wrath."[136]

Relationship of the Church with Political Power

The Orthodox Church sanctifies not only the governed but also the governors. In fact, the Church considers all baptized Christians to be its children, whether they are conscientious Orthodox Christians or are indifferent or even hostile to the Church. And if they are not yet baptized Orthodox Christians, they are nevertheless icons of God and, therefore, potentially children of the Church, so the Church embraces them with motherly love, depending on the degree to which they themselves are willingly receptive to such love.[137]

The Church can be seen as a hospital that heals souls in relation to both the present world and the future eternal one. A hospital naturally wants to have good relations with the state, so that it can carry out its work smoothly for the benefit even of the state itself, which is interested in having spiritually healthy citizens. Ensuring, at the highest level, these good and close relations can theoretically be achieved in two alternative ways: either by the Church exercising control over the state or by the Church exercising influence over the state. According to our view, the Church should seek to have the maximum possible influence on the state, and at the same time the maximum possible independence from the state (including, of course, financial independence), and at the same time the maximum possible, or rather absolute, abstention from state power because the kingdom of heaven is not "of this world."[138] The Gospel indeed teaches us that Christ denied all worldly authority. He did not succumb to the temptation of Satan to "give" Him power over all the kingdoms of the world, and He left the enthusiastic group of people who wanted to crown Him secular king, after the miracle of the multiplication of the loaves and the fish.[139] However, He did not refuse to speak to eminent people of His time about the Gospel, as well as bless them with His miracles.[140] Paul also asked to be tried by Caesar with the obvious purpose of confessing Christ before the "global ruler" of that time.[141] From Church history, we see that the Church encourages every king to be benevolent in Christ.[142] The Church regards that the exercise of state political power is not considered incompatible with holiness, as it is clear from many examples including the canonization of Emperor Constantine, who is even considered as equal to an apostle, due to the exercise of secular power in a Christian spirit and his decisive role in legalizing and spreading Christianity. Another example is the canonization of Tsar Vladimir of Novgorod who was instrumental in inspiring the Christianization of Kievan Rus, as well as Tsar Nicholas II and his immediate family for their meekness, patience, and heroism in the face of Bolshevik persecution and execution.[143]

Political power and holiness are not considered mutually incompatible, but on the other hand every exercise of power inevitably involves an element of division between rulers and subjects which, to some extent, poses an obstacle or difficulty in respect of the communion of love expressed by the Church. Perhaps for this reason, among others, the Church rightly does not allow the participation of clergy in the exercise of power in a secular, official capacity.[144]

We believe that the combination, "maximum possible influence and zero institutionalized state power" in respect of Church–State relations can be applied in practice, on the one hand with the maximum possible advisory presence of the Church (through lay representatives appointed by her) in state bodies and state decision-making centers and, on the other hand, with her total absence and abstinence from institutionalized executive state structures.[145] In other words, the Church cannot support the assumption of secular offices by the clergy, but this would not prevent the presence of lay representatives appointed by the Church in all state branches (executive, legislative, judicial) in an advisory and not executive role. This arrangement can be considered to be in line with the system of "symphony," where the state and the Church preserve their independence, while at the same time maintaining a close relationship and cooperation, and by both recognizing Jesus Christ as the supreme authority.[146] The proposal for the participation of Church-appointed advisors at all levels of government aims to institutionalize the relationship or harmonious coexistence between the state and the Church, so that this relationship is not overly dependent on the policies of the leader or ruling party which happens to be in power at a particular period.

The system of "symphony" avoids, on the one hand, the system of theocracy, where the state submits to the Church, and on the other, the strictly secular state, where there is a complete and dogmatic separation of Church and State. In both cases, there is a risk of secularization. In the first, the Church becomes a state and authority in a way that is not in line with the Gospel, while in the case of a strict separation of State and Church, the Church could, in an extreme form of separation, appear to be like an association or private secular institution, and faith in God could be reduced to a private, individual, secular affair.[147]

Of course, we must emphasize that the separation of Church and State can take various forms and nuances. At its worst, the Church is completely marginalized, and is, as has already been said, something like a club. At best, it has a symbolic presence through protocol at state events and is also a kind of state within a state because of the great trust and honor with which it is invested by the people. In this second sense, the separation of Church and State does not lead to the marginalization of the Church but rather protects her from subordination by the state, which may take place if the latter abuses its predominant position by taking advantage of the institutional presence of the Church within the State as a branch of the State apparatus, and in this way seeks to impose itself on her. This could happen when the Church becomes a legal entity under public law as is the case of Greece,[148] resulting in the restriction of her freedom through a coercive embrace by the state, as it is subject to government control as a state body.[149] Better (but not perfect) conditions of freedom of movement compared to this system are provided by a constitutionally guaranteed legal status of independence such as in Cyprus,[150] allowing the Church to function in some way as a "state within a state" in the sense that the state cannot intervene in the affairs of the Church as if it were a state or semi-state organization.

Nevertheless, it would be wrong for the Church to support the separation of Church and State, even in its best and mildest form, because that would indirectly be tantamount to secularism. It would be as if the Church herself were saying: "I'll stay in my world and the State in its world." While the theologically correct approach is: The whole world was a Church before the fall, and the purpose of the Church after Pentecost is to restore the world to its former glorious position as Church. It is of course a matter of discernment how the Church will pursue this aim, but on the other hand any support of the Church toward the principle of separation of State and Church would indirectly constitute an *a priori* negation of this very aim.[151]

A Person-centered System of Government—Monarchy

Notwithstanding the above positions regarding the relationship between the Church and political power, the question arises as to whether the Church favors or should favor a particular system of government. Or with what criteria should the Church approach the issue of choosing or proposing the most appropriate system of government? Such a system, in our opinion, should have a strong person-centered dimension, since in the Church "truth" is neither an idea nor an ideology, but a person (Jesus Christ).[152] Of course, in the eyes of the Church, any kind of government is better than anarchy. This does not mean, however, that in the eyes of the Church all forms of government are the same.[153] Nor, on the other hand, does the Church dogmatically support, i.e., based on theological doctrine, a specific system of government, regardless of social conditions,[154] as such a dogmatization of a secular issue would be equivalent to an indirect secularization of the Church, in a way which betokens rigidity and lack of discernment.

However, the Church could give some guidelines, drawing inspiration from the reality and truth emanating from the person (as opposed to impersonal ideas), and by adapting to (but not conforming to) the prevailing social conditions. The state should, in our opinion, be one that upholds the rule of law, that is, subject to the (inevitably) impersonal law, but with a strong human-centered dimension in order to compensate for the aforementioned impersonality of the law. The right combination must be found between the impersonal law of the state and the personal ruler of the state. This leader should be strong and not a puppet of hidden and impersonal political-economic interests. On the other hand, he should be subject to the law so as not to inspire terror in a way that might reduce or even eliminate the possibility of building a personal-communal relationship with his subjects. The Church should, therefore, favor a person-centered system of government where the government has a clear personalized identity in terms of both powers and duties. But "person" presupposes "communion" with one's "neighbor" and communion with one's neighbor essentially means love. This person must be receptive of love and capable to love, and love presupposes a relationship based on respect and in the absence of fear. Because fear is hell.[155] That is why the ruler must be subject to the law and not be above the law, because the rule of law is the main counterweight and antidote to the terror of lawlessness. We believe that a person-centered, rule-of-law democracy is what is needed to promote and enhance an advanced form of society which we may call "communion of persons." Democracy and the rule of law should strengthen the communal and personal dimension of society and not the mass, impersonal dimension.[156] Democracy and the rule of law, in this sense, should not be detached from society, but should be an integral part of it, and be a means of strengthening the communion of love between the people (horizontal relationship) and between the people and the rulers (vertical relationship).

We believe that the Monarchy offers this person-centered compensation to the impersonal rule of law, provided that it is adapted to democracy, and subject to the rule of law and parliamentary and judicial control. A kingdom that does not undermine democracy but on the contrary legitimizes, strengthens, and enriches it by giving it a personal hypostasis and also stability.[157] The king should be elected by the people[158] as a life-long leader (up to a certain retirement age to be determined by law, e.g., 75 years). There should not be any class, hereditary, or economic criteria for a candidate to be electable by the people. But he must be an Orthodox Christian and be anointed and crowned king within an ecclesiastical sacrament with the participation of the archbishop. This coronation will function as a complementary and reinforcing legitimacy of the king's power, in addition to the popular mandate he receives through his democratic election.[159]

As the bishop is theologically "in the form and place of Christ,"[160] the same should apply by analogy to the king except for the sacramental role which he does not possess as a layman.[161] He does not perform sacraments but his coronation and quasi-religious role adds dignity to the state and provides motivation to himself to imitate and follow the sacrificial path of Christ as a servant of God and of the people.[162] The king's presence is in place but not instead of Christ. He should be there to contribute, from a non-ecclesiastical position, in inspiring the people in the realization that Christ is "the head of all principality and authority."[163]

The king may also unite and "personalize" the nation, as an antidote against its nationalistic ideologicization. On the other hand, the king's Christian identity should provide a safety net against any temptation of self-deification, an act which would essentially constitute a negation of his personhood and his ability to commune with his people. Such self-aggrandizement may take place either for the sake or under the pretext of ideology (such as the phenomenon of Stalinism) or for the sake or under the pretext of self-deification (as sought by the emperors of the Roman Empire before its Christianization as well as Roman popes after the Schism). By trying to deify himself, the leader depersonalizes himself through self-exaltation: with this move he builds a wall of fear and terror between him and the people, blocking communion, because communion of persons presupposes a relationship characterized by mutual respect and love. Without communion there is no personhood (and without personhood there is no communion). The subordination of the king to the law of the state serves the same purpose of preventing his self-aggrandizement to a level where it prevents communion with his subjects, in love and respect.

With the king's lifetime term in office (not literally but until an age to be decided by law), democracy is not undermined but strengthened. Democracy means power to the people, and this presupposes that the people are worthy of trust. So the people should be considered responsible enough and trustworthy to elect their leader with extreme seriousness, and not superficially. Just as in marriage one makes a lifelong commitment, so it should be with political elections: one should choose a lifelong leader. With the same seriousness.

The people are therefore called upon to elect their leader, who must have the benefit of time, to implement policies that may take years to bear fruit. The leader/king will consider the real interests of the people, not how he will be pleasing to them so that he can win the next elections. He will not be subject to the pressure of populism and the temptation of sacrificing the public interest for the sake of party and factional interests.

The Relationship of the Church with Ideologies and Parties

According to the Orthodox faith, truth is not an idea or ideology, but a Person and a communion of persons.[164] The search for truth in ideas, by overriding or subordinating the person, seems to be in line with Platonic philosophy but not in line with the Christian Orthodox view, according to which truth is a Person and not an idea: "Then, the Holy Fathers, answering the questions of the ancient Greek philosophers about the essence of beings, spoke about the so-called reasons of beings, which are not the ideas of Plato ... but the uncreated energy of God that sustains all creation."[165] Also characteristic is the Gospel passage, where Pilate asks Christ "What is truth?" a question to which Christ does not answer, a fact which, according to the Church Fathers, testifies that the question itself was wrong, since the correct question would be "Who [and not what] is truth?"[166]

The idea is, therefore, impersonal in nature. If the person is not the master of ideology, but instead identifies with or subordinates himself to impersonal ideology, then that person reduces his own status as a person because he ceases to think freely and undermines his own ability to commune with the other person. But if he uses or utilizes the idea as a means of effecting the communion, then the idea takes its rightful place as a servant to the communion of persons. The person, by communing, strengthens and authenticates his existence as a person.[167]

But there is also a false communion or socialization of the idea which does not signify a person-centered communion but an impersonal massification. When the idea is wrapped in ideology, it is "communicated" both massively and divisively, not for the purpose of achieving communion but rather for the purpose of dividing society, through deliberate polarization so as to offer the supporter of an ideology an artificial and false sense of identity, which distinguishes and alienates him from his neighbor instead of helping him achieve communion with him.[168]

The more all-embracing the ideology, the more likely it is to enhance a false sense of individuality as opposed to personal communion.[169] A claim of comprehensiveness is not conducive to communion but, on the contrary, leads to a strengthening of non-communal individuality within the "security" provided by the collective. This is provided of course that the "opposing" ideology is also present to give the "necessary" distinctiveness to the "opposing" ideologies, thus reinforcing the false sense of collective and individual identity offered to their supporters, and giving them a false pretext for avoiding or bypassing the "risk" of true, non-ideological, person-centered communion. Thus, ideological comprehensiveness and ideological polarization constitute a common axis of strengthening the impersonal individual at the expense of personal communion. In other words, a common axis of delusion since the axis of "comprehensiveness and polarization" is the antithesis of the axis of "communion and union," which is based on the person (not on the individual)[170] and which is a prerequisite of truth.[171]

What is required, then, is that any idea be immersed and baptized in the waters of communion or society, to wash away any inherently divisive ideological stains. But how is this achieved in practice? First of all, by trying to present or share one's ideas in a way that neither excludes nor imposes participation on any person. The first step in this effort is to avoid, to the greatest possible degree, the political labeling or veiling based on "right and left wing" schematization, as this veil itself creates an obstacle to the communion of persons. In a way it is a veil hiding a person's face, erecting a wall between citizens, and revealing an inward desire to distance oneself from neighbor so that everyone can keep their self-contained ideological identity, thus hindering the communion of persons, and even leading to delusion, as truth can be achieved only in communion.[172] The attachment of a person to ideology is therefore a socially divisive act, and therefore anticommunal. To be right wing, one "needs" to have a leftist "opposing" him (and vice versa) and inwardly is happy to label him "left wing," in order to be positioned to the right (or left) of him or, in the worst case, to justify his acquiring power over him.

Here, of course, a distinction should be made: on the one hand, the *description* of a policy as right wing and left wing in a way which could be considered merely as a tool of political analysis, and, on the other hand, the identification, that is, the derivation of identity from the "right–left" schematization. In the latter case, we do not have merely a description, but a *prescription* of a way of thinking, a voluntary relinquishing of freedom of thought purposefully leading to an artificial division of society: to a dichotomy of "us versus you," in a way that contradicts the spirit of the Gospel.

Devotion to an ideology, in its most extreme manifestation, can also be motivated by self-deification. The desire of the individual to identify with an ideology as an "immortal idea" and through it to "achieve" his own immortality, bypassing the need for loving communion with the God-man Christ and neighbor. Or even, for the sake of ideology, man can declare war on God, seeking the replacement or elimination of his Church. Indeed, within Marxist states there was a clear attempt to exalt communist ideology to the status of religion, to an absolute faith attempting even to displace God from society.

Even democracy, if elevated to the status of absolute ideology, can lead to tyranny, based on this equation: (a) democracy means power to the people, (b) power of the people is promoted by unity and cohesion of the people, (c) unity of the people is enhanced by their economic equality, (d) in order to preserve the power of the people, they should be protected from those among them who do not support equality, therefore the operation of any party which does not support the above positions is prohibited (e) hence, there should be a one-party political system, with all other parties declared illegal! From this perfectly logical equation, and from historical experience, it appears that the absolutization of an impersonal idea (even that of democracy) and its exaltation above the person and society may lead to inhuman and antisocial oppression.[173]

In an apparently milder (but perhaps more insidious) form, ideology may seek to subordinate the Church to nationalist ideology and use it as a tool to serve political and ideological goals. And this can happen even if at first sight there is no subordination but elevation. An example of the above would be an ideology expressed by various slogans such as: "Religion, Fatherland, Family." Prima facie, God is rightly placed above the other two institutions, yet He is at the same time relativized and conformed to worldly institutions in a way that betokens subordination to this triad, even if He takes first place in it.

The Church cannot conform to any ideology. In particular, her aversion to communist ideology should not lead her to the "opposite" (supposedly) right-wing or nationalist ideology, as if Christ was a right-wing nationalist! It could indeed be said that the greatest service to the atheist left would be the positioning and conformation of the Church with the right. (But as we have stated already, inwardly this may be exactly the purpose of the right-wing nationalist because he "needs" the left in order to confirm his identity as a right-winger). While the correct way to weaken the atheist left is not by the Church entrenching herself behind an "opposing" ideology, but to try to inspire the people to liberate themselves from the chains of ideology, using Christian Orthodox *Personology* (teaching regarding the human person) as a therapeutic medicine. Ideology is the opposite of "Personology" espoused by the Church, where the emphasis is not on any idea or ideology, not even on the ideas or teachings of Christ, but on communion with Christ Himself as a person (within the community of his Church), leading, not to idealization or ideologicization, but to the deification of man in divine grace. One could indeed argue that the man who wants to believe in Christ and at the same time continues to identify and remain attached to a specific ideology, acts in a way that contradicts the evangelical saying: "No servant can serve two masters, for either he will hate the one and love the other, or else he will be loyal to the one and despise the other ...."[174]

And this applies even if the "right-left" schematization in some cases does not have a clear meaning or content. Because just by the act of calling oneself either right-wing or left-wing, a disposition of identification with an impersonal idea has been manifested, regardless of the meaning one attaches to these terms. In other words, this identification constitutes a use of a veil of either "right-wing" or "left-wing" with potentially anti-communal or antisocial consequences. We are thus not interested in the questions "what does right-wing mean?" or "what does left-wing mean?" Because whatever they mean, or even if they don't mean anything at all, by the act of calling oneself (either an individual or a party) "right" or "left," and by identifying with these abstractions, one has already manifested an unwholesome attraction to the impersonal, an addiction to the ideological veil, and a potential desire to reject Christian Orthodox person-centeredness.

By encouraging the people to transcend the "right-left" schematization, the Church also contributes to the prevention of fanaticism and discord within society. Because one who declares himself either "right-wing" or "left-wing" can, potentially, become extreme right-wing or left-wing, or he may inwardly take pleasure when extreme right or extreme left positions are expressed either in speech or actions. One can easily follow the slippery road leading to the extremes once he is already addicted to a certain degree to impersonal and depersonalizing ideological attachment. In other words, he can become a fanatic and deluded to such an extent as to place his ideology above the interests of his motherland and, in the worst case, even above God. By contrast, by overcoming attachment to ideologies, society has greater freedom to experience Christian Orthodox spirituality with the Person at its core, strengthening the people spiritually and morally, and allowing them to unleash their creative power in a path of progress and achievement.

Of course, it is quite possible for a right- or left-wing party to have better political standpoints than a non-ideological, center party on a particular issue or even on a majority of issues. It is also possible that voting for a right-wing or left-wing party in a particular election may be appropriate. Nevertheless, the expression of the Church's general preference for parties that do not identify with either the right or the left, would serve a necessary, in our view, purpose, which is to emphasize the freedom of the person to shift politically on a specific issue either to the right or to the left if he considers that it is in the interest of his country to do so. This approach is in harmony with the Pauline saying: "I have become all things to all men, that I might by all means save some."[175] Such a freedom would not be available to a person attached to an ideology (whether a citizen or a politician) because ideology becomes a binding force and an integral part of his identity.

Of course, there is no question of the Church closing the door on any person or group of people because of their political affiliations or ideology. But it does have, in our view, an obligation to offer to the people a de minimis political guidance. We believe that it is somewhat paradoxical and unnatural for the Church to claim: "we can guide God's people on every issue ... except on politics!" It is better for the believer to familiarize himself with Christian Orthodox Political Philosophy consisting of basic principles which he could, if he so desires, adopt them and use them as a tool of political analysis and interpretation.[176]

Of course, we are not arguing that the Church should found a political party because that would constitute *conformation with* this world. On the other hand, we do not support the view that the Church should be indifferent to politics because that would constitute a denial of the possibility of *sanctification of* the world, and such a denial would, in fact, constitute another form of worldly conformation as it would reduce the Church to the sphere of abstract, ideological, utopian beliefs.

Church and Human Rights

Within and among traditionally Christian-majority nations the realization that the protection and implementation of human rights is a prerequisite for the existence and progress of a society and an important social achievement is quite evident and beyond doubt. Human rights, seen from the point of view of the Church and in the light of Orthodox theology, should be interpreted and inspired by the Orthodox person-in-communion-centered tradition, and in particular by the teaching that, as God is one and, at the same time, a trinity of Persons (subject to the monarchy of the Father), so human society (i.e., mankind created in God's image) should and could ideally be one and at the same time a multitude of persons. Just as the existence, in otherness, of the three Persons of the Holy Trinity does not undermine the oneness of God, so the existence, in otherness, of each and every person who together constitute one society should ideally not undermine the oneness of society.[177]

Human rights should serve this twofold goal: unity in diversity, and diversity in unity. According to this approach, there is no foundation in the idea of oppressing the person for the sake of society because the person is an integral part and a living cell of the body of society, so the oppression of the person is equivalent to the oppression of society itself. Just as a body has many members, so society has many members that make up one body, so the pain and sickness (or oppression) of one member of the body affects the general condition of the whole body.[178]

Could one claim that the above view is in harmony with the ideology of communism or Marxism? We believe that there is an essential difference: Marx on the one hand presents man as a social being like Christian Orthodoxy but, on the other, he presents him as being subject of the social class to which he belongs, and indeed to an extent reaching ontological dimensions. In other words, Marxism presents man not as a social being but as a class being. With the classes constituting deep, and in fact unbridgeable divisions. It could be said that classes according to Marxism are antisocial divisions of society to an extent that there can be no communion between these classes, in stark contrast to the potential communion with God offered to all espoused by Orthodoxy. According to Marx, union and communion within society can be achieved through class struggle leading to revolutionary violence and the destruction of one class by another, thus bringing about a classless society. Revolutionary violence, however, is not in line with the Gospel, save, perhaps, for exceptional situations after all avenues of compromise have been exhausted due to the intransigence of the oppressing side. From a Christian point of view, it is unacceptable for revolutionary violence to be an integral part of philosophical and ideological systems, as is clearly the case in Marxism where compromise between classes is clearly rejected.[179] Violence means pain, hatred, death, humiliation, and much more—can a true and healthy society be born from the antisocial seed of violence and revolution, that is, of civil war?[180] Experience has shown that Marxist regimes borne of revolution continued using violence and the threat of use of force after the revolution to ensure that society complied with the absolute authority of the Communist Party.[181] This is clearly at odds with Christian Orthodoxy according to which the human relations within a society presuppose freedom and love as opposed to violent coercion.

Thus it would be more correct to say that the communist, Marxist view of society, in spite of some superficial similarities, is not in accord with the Orthodox understanding of freedom to engender into unity and oneness by love, but rather it is manifested and characterized by an inherently conflictual model of class divisions and hatred where classes are engaged in a struggle for survival and dominance leading to civil war, as a result of which the proletarian class will triumph and create a classless society.

Based on this Orthodox view of love and freedom, the legislator should seek to provide the person with those appropriate rights but also obligations that will help him in his self-realization as a communal being, that will help him to live in love with neighbor and society. It is also understood that the legislator should endeavor, without suppressing the freedom of the person, to encourage or at least not hinder the person's communion with God. Therefore, in a Christian society, rights should not be meant as a shield of protection from society (let alone from God) but a shield of protection from "anti-society," that is, from the antisocial behavior of either some of our fellow citizens or the state itself—when it acts in an undemocratic and oppressive manner. When, the state does not consider the sensitivities, dignity, and needs of the person.

From a Christian point of view, a legislator's democratic character is a good quality, which betokens respect for the dignity of one's neighbor.[182] But something further is also needed: the recognition of man as an image of God. Based on this recognition, the Christian legislator views the rights and obligations he grants and imposes on the citizen as medicine to help cure (as far as possible) his illness as a result of the fall, rendering him a perfect, communal person (vertically in relation to God and horizontally in relation to his neighbor) just as God created him, in His image and likeness. However, the legislator, acting in a therapeutic capacity, should also be aware that without the "patient's" cooperation he cannot cure him no matter how effective the medicines at his disposal are. This is where democracy comes in to play so that patient consent is necessary and sought after. The legislator cannot impose the criminalization of any sin to force the person to become perfect. Coercion and oppression are not in harmony with the brotherhood of man as envisaged by the Gospel. Adultery and pre-marital sexual relations are a "right" today in all Christian-majority states, and it would not be wise for the state to criminalize these sins because, in the present circumstances, society would consider such a measure as overly oppressive and invasive of the personal lives of citizens, causing an antisocial or anti-communal division and schism between legislator and society.

On the other hand, the legislator should help the person realize that the perception that sin is a right is not a healthy one. In other words, the Christian legislator should also be characterized by a healthy conservatism. In particular, where an existing state of affairs, consistent with Christian theology and ethics, is accepted by the majority of society, such as the criminalization of abortion, the prohibition of euthanasia, the prohibition of transsexualism (especially for minors), the prohibition of same-sex marriage, or the incapacity of same-sex couples to adopt children, then in these matters, the legislature should not overturn these legal restrictions by invoking an artificial need to protect sinful human "rights" of minority groups, to the (spiritual) detriment of these groups themselves as well as to the right of the majority to have a say on the fundamental question concerning what kind of society they and their families want to live in.

At the socioeconomic level, similar conservatism and resistance should be demonstrated by the Christian legislator regarding the erosion of the welfare state and social rights and goods, such as free and high-level education and healthcare, since these are goods which are directly related to Christian charity and love. In other words, the Christian legislator should in no way hesitate to agree with left-wing parties, where their positions are in line with Christian charity and love, even if they have different perspectives, motives, or aims.

In addition to a personal and communal-centered approach, the culture of respect for and enforcement of human rights should also have a universal and international dimension. Simply put, a government cannot, on the one hand, be civilized, law-abiding, and properly behaved at home, respecting the dignity of its citizens, but regarding the outside world act like a real barbarian, indulging in illegal and highly destructive military operations in violation of international law.

Church and Person-centered Economic Policy

The economy is undoubtedly an integral part of politics. Economic policy cannot be pursued either with the use of ideological blindfolds and hallucinogens or guided by petty party and political interests. The stable rule of a king as a lifelong leader (until his compulsory retirement, for example, after reaching his 75th birthday) will prevent, to the greatest possible degree, the subordination of economic policy to partisan and ideological interests, as well as the sacrifice of long-term national interests for the benefit of petty political or ideological expediencies.

Economic policy is such an important issue for the happiness, progress, and prosperity of the people that the Church cannot afford to be absent and silent or to confine herself to trite generalizations. Such silence may leave a void that could be filled by other theories and philosophies that may be opposed to the teaching of the Church. Of course, the Church is not an agency of economic experts invested with the power and duty to formulate a comprehensive economic policy for the benefit or on behalf of a particular government, but it can provide inspiration to any given economic experts based on her principles and worldview regarding society as more than the sum of all its members, which may serve as an antidote, counterweight, and deterrent to the detachment of economic theory from society.

How can the Church's teaching on the person and communion be used as a source of principled analysis in the field of economic policy? A good start would be to attempt to describe pre-fall paradise in economic terms. Then apply it, within the limits of realistic feasibility, to the post-fall world after duly taking into account, on the one hand, the post-fall "nature" of man, and on the other, his inherent yearning to return to his pre-fall beauty and harmony of loving communion with God and neighbor.

What is then pre-fall paradise? It is the perfect harmony of God, man, and nature. Economic policy, even if it is inspired by Theology, is inevitably obliged to concentrate on the second aspect which relates to harmony among people which, of course, does not exclude nor hinders communion with God but, on the contrary, it facilitates it.[183] Hence, economic policy must serve the harmony of society. It should help in the direction of wealth creation, and this wealth should promote the relations within society. Economic policy should combine in the best possible way the freedom of the human person and equality between the members of society as a basic catalyst for leading it toward the lost paradisical estate, in so far as this is possible in the present age where sin remains present. Because, the more one feels oppressed or disadvantaged compared to others, the more difficult it is for him to have love for them, as the more he relates to them, the more self-conscious he will feel of his disadvantageous position. This is so, especially if he feels that he has been unjustly treated by others; this is likely to create a rift and a trauma which hinder the relationship between the real or perceived victim and the real or perceived victimizer or privileged person. The sense of injustice relates primarily to the poor, but not exclusively. It could also apply to a wealthy person if he feels unjustly treated as a result of an arbitrary confiscation of his property or by an imbalanced taxation system which may act as a brake on creativity and productivity.

A perfect human-centered, sociocentric economic system is therefore that which combines economic equality and economic freedom in the best possible way or even in the best mutually reinforcing way. Financial freedom for the production of wealth, but wealth that should to the greatest possible degree, be shared with others and not remain with the person who won it with "his" intelligence or "his" ability or even with "his" hard work." Ideally, he should overcome his individualism for the sake of love for his fellow man, and deliver his wealth with joy and without pressure, recognizing that his talents that allowed him to create wealth, as well as the wealth itself, do not really belong to him but are gifts from God offered for use by the holder as a trustee for the benefit of his neighbor.[184] In other words, the perfect economic system could be expressed, prima facie, with the following principle: maximum possible incentive to produce wealth and at the same time maximum possible redistribution of wealth for the benefit of all the people.

But this two-dimensional principle must be combined with a third dimension or parameter which is to achieve the goal of maximizing the re-utilization or reinvestment of wealth in order to maintain, sustain, and produce more wealth in the future for the common good, as well as with a fourth dimension or parameter which is the achievement of the goal of maximizing the wealth of the state treasury, so that the state can carry out projects for the common good, create conditions for further prosperity, take measures to enhance the welfare state, protect the environment, strengthen defense, etc. As has been said before, the state can play a very powerful, catalytic role in promoting interpersonal, communal relationships within society, through the feeling of security, prosperity, and identity it can offer to its citizens, and through the sense of love it can instill in them for the state itself as a communal body.

On the basis of the above, taking into account all the above parameters, the most perfect economic system can be considered to be the one that ensures:

a) the maximum possible prosperity of the state,
b) the maximum possible prosperity of the citizens,
c) the maximum possible investment and reinvestment of wealth to serve the above objectives;

d) the maximum possible redistribution of wealth in society in pursuit of the social equality of citizens.

In a nutshell, these principles could be summarized with the following axiom: person-and-commune-centered creation, redistribution, investment of maximum possible wealth.

VOLUNTARY PAYMENT TO THE STATE BEYOND AND ABOVE TAX OBLIGATIONS

The goal of maximizing wealth creation and investment and the prevention of capital flight to other countries that may have lower taxes is served by low taxation. The goal of the fairest or most equitable distribution of wealth could be served by high tax rates, which is aimed at the wealth of the rich. The choice of tax rate should reflect a balance between these two competing objectives. But regardless of this balance, the financial prosperity of the state could be promoted if there was some way of voluntary, and not only via taxation, funding of the state by its wealthy citizens, either with direct state funding or, indirectly, with financial aid to the poor through charitable gifts securing tax deductions. The Christian spirit of charity can play an important and catalytic role in this endeavor, especially with regard to the aspect of charity toward the poor. As for direct funding of the state, some positive incentives could be explored to motivate a wealthy person to agree, without pressure or coercion, to contribute to the state part of his wealth, over and above his necessary compliance with taxation.[185]

Such a measure could be the issuing of government bonds to raise capital, as well as to offer non-material incentives to those who voluntarily contribute funds (the amount of which will be determined by law) to the state treasury in addition to their tax obligations, offering to these benefactors official advisory posts, according to their professional and academic credentials. That is, the state could set up state councils, with advisory rather than executive powers, specialized in various fields, such as economics, entrepreneurship, education, culture, the members of which could be contributors to the state treasury in addition to their tax obligations. In other words, this system could essentially enable the purchase of advisory positions by the wealthy for themselves provided that they have a clean criminal record, a high level of education, that they are in compliance with tax obligations, and are free of party membership. Such an institution could promote a harmonious coexistence of democracy and aristocracy by reducing the inclination, on the one hand, to masonic membership, as well as the inclination, on the other, to party affiliation and divisive, antisocial, ideological attachment. Hence, it is an aristocracy that puts itself at the service of the person and society, i.e., does not oppress the person and society through its wealth, but invests this wealth for the acquisition of advisory positions, while at the same time strengthening the state treasury for the benefit of society.

But is this a real incentive or will these advisory bodies end up being just "talking shops" with pointless discussions and with members' money having been thrown into an impersonal and faceless governmental black hole? As a person-centered counterweight to this possibility, these councils should be chaired by the head of state himself. Thus, the fear that these advisory bodies will become coffee shops will be reduced due to the special weight and prestige offered by the presence and participation of the head of state (especially if he is a king), who will ensure the proper utilization of these councils for the benefit of his government and society in general.

Private v Public Sector

In conjunction with the above four principles/criteria for wealth creation and distribution, which are based on the philosophy of interpersonal harmony, the right combination of the private and public sectors in the economy should also be chosen, so that this mix serves the same purpose of wealth creation which is conducive to strengthening interpersonal communal bonds within society. In order to pursue this purpose, the applicable criterion for the correct balance between private and public sector within the economy could be expressed as follows: how does an economic enterprise or organization become as productive as possible—not as an end in itself—not by circumventing and bypassing interpersonal harmony—but through its strengthening and promotion? When is such an organization more likely to strike a correct balance between, on

the one hand, maximum productivity and, on the other, minimal impersonality (or alienation) between customer and owner? If it is within the
private or public sector?

If we take as an example the case of restaurants or barber shops, we
believe that if these were generally state-owned then such a state of affairs
would give rise to most evident impersonality and alienation in comparison to the case of their being private. But if we are talking about airports,
airlines, water supply, electricity companies, commercial banks, then the
answer might be different. It could be said that the person using these
services is more comfortable doing so on the basis of his status as "citizen"
rather than "customer," and naturally feels more familiar with the state,
public, and (ideally) social control of these organizations than with their
private operation, given that there is a clear relationship of dependence
of the citizen vis-à-vis such organizations. The nationalization (partial or
total) of corporate giants can in this sense provide a communal shield and
antidote to the covert (impersonal) exercise of power through corporate
wealth that secures political influence without democratic legitimacy or
social (communal) control.[186] This is especially true if the corporate giant
is controlled by foreign interests, an element that certainly tends to lead
toward the weakening of social (communal) control because interpersonal communal harmony, as has been described previously, presupposes
a common place or locality where it is to be found.[187]

As a general principle, the larger and more "dependency-creating"
an organization is from the point of view of the citizen, or the greater its
importance for the economy, for politics, for culture, or for state security
and sovereignty, the more necessary it is for it to be fully or partially under
state-public (social) control.[188] Or at least in some sectors where it is not
clear which of the two options is more impersonal and beyond social control, it would be wise for the state to ensure a balance between the private
and public sector, such as in the areas of media, education, and health.

STATE SECTOR WORK SECURITY

It should be acknowledged, however, that although the policy of
nationalization of some corporations or sectors may be implemented

with the purpose of bringing these under the control of the community, this course of action may be accompanied by side effects that may contradict the very rationale of the said approach. This can happen when a state employee hides behind a state veil, looks down on the citizen, and underperforms at work, taking advantage of and abusing the greater job security generally provided by the state sector. The relative job security within the public sector is a privilege that does not exist to the same degree in the private sector, but its existence is necessary so that there is no risk of dismissal of a civil servant due to his political affiliations and his replacement with one with greater loyalty to the party which happens to be in power. But this privilege and benefit may be abused leading to reduced productivity and diligence. The absence of incentive to generate wealth in the public sector due to the lack of self-interest can lead to the same result. The solution, however, is not necessarily privatization (where such privatization would be an even more powerful catalyst toward anticommunal depersonalization), but rather the targeted treatment of this very problem of lack of incentive. We propose the promotion, as a necessary counterweight to this factor, the increase of *dis*incentive *not* to work, through the imposition of a mild form of military discipline and organization in the public sector, in terms of a strict, immediate, and direst internal accountability and disciplinary system, a pyramidal structure of administration and a strict culture against political perforation within the public sector's institutional boundaries.[189] Such an internal "militarization" of the state sector will not pose a threat to the conscientious civil servant or public sector employee, but to the one who purposefully and cynically seeks a parasitic life at the expense of society or who seeks to devalue and divide the public sector through political partisanship.

This approach could also be a disincentive to appointments in the public sector on the basis of party affiliations (within the framework of a party clientele system) due to the balanced removal of the attractiveness of these public sector posts, as a result of the military-type discipline that will characterize the work culture. To serve the same purpose of a balanced removal of the attractiveness of public sector employments, the measure of correlating public sector wages with private sector wages could be additionally implemented in such a way that public sector positions (respectively, by analogy, and on average) will not only cease to be higher-paid than those of the respective private sector but, on the contrary, will be lower-paid, albeit slightly.

Hopefully, these measures will prevent or at least drastically reduce one of the worst kinds of work discrimination imaginable: the appointment (or promotion) of persons based on party lists, a state of affairs which constitutes a blow to the dignity of both the successful and unsuccessful candidate, and a rift within the harmony of society through the triumph of impersonal ideological partisanship.

EMPLOYER–EMPLOYEE RELATIONSHIP WITHIN THE PRIVATE SECTOR

On the basis of a personal-communal approach, the distinction between employer and employee should exist in the private sector but in such a way that it is conducive to unity and harmony within the workplace. Equality is conducive to person-and-commune-based unity provided that it is not forced, rebellious, and anarchic. The democratization of the working place[190] could be conducive to person-and-commune-based harmony and equality provided that it is not based on impersonal ideology. Within this spirit, such democratization of the workplace could be pursued via non-partisan, non-ideological trade-unionism (where party membership of trade union officials is prohibited) and where trade unions are, to the maximum possible degree, enterprise-based[191] (conducive to harmony of persons within a common place) rather than sector-based (inevitably entailing supra-local impersonality).

STATE CURRENCY

Based on the same rationale of subjecting the economy to social control, the currency of an Orthodox-majority state should also be national, as a basic tool for exercising economic policy,[192] unless the choice for the use of a supra-national currency is made within the framework of national self-transcendence for the purpose of a union with other nations on the basis of Christian Orthodox civilization. Based on the same reasoning of utilizing the economy as an instrument for strengthening the state and society, the economy should have a strong local, national dimension, so that its foundations are unassailable by outside international pressures that are beyond social control. In other words, it must be sufficiently independent, with strong agricultural and industrial sectors in addition to the sectors of tourism and professional services, which are more vulnerable to external factors, pressures, crises, and developments.

FREE MARKET AND FREE TRADE V STATE INTERVENTION AND PROTECTIONISM

In extension of the above views which are based on the endeavor to subject the economy to the needs of society, we believe that the economy must be a free market economy to the extent that it serves the interests of the community, which inevitably is based on a common territory or locality. In this sense, a market is actually free in the personal-communal sense when it promotes the strengthening of interpersonal bonds within the community in a spirit of unity in diversity, by attending to the material and psychological needs of the members of that society. The market is indeed a very useful instrument in the hands of society for its material well-being, for wealth creation, and for business activity and creativity.

The free market may cease to serve the community in a case where it falls under the control of supra-communal or para-communal interests which may be of a monopolistic or oligopolistic nature. In such a case, the state, as an instrument of the community should intervene on its behalf either by nationalizing monopolies or cutting them down to size, i.e., subjecting them to the community by the application of anti-monopoly laws.

But these interests may also be of a foreign nature and thus, prima facie, have a supra-communal nature, beyond the control of the community which presupposes a common place, and this common place is naturally the common state which, as has been argued earlier, invests this common place with a communal and personal dimension. A state-based approach does not exclude international cooperation and even harmony based on free international trade, but subjects it to the needs of the state-based community to which priority is given. In other words, according to this approach the local market must retain its local character in order to retain its freedom, through protectionist measures which aim at protecting local businesses (provided that they are not monopolies). International trade should be encouraged only where there is a gap in the local market which cannot be adequately filled by local businesses.

Of course, the concept of common territory or locality can be expanded in some cases to cover a common market, such as the European Union. Such an extension of the concept of common market, implicitly or explicitly, presupposes a commitment or desire to create a common state, which as has been argued earlier, from an Orthodox point of view, presupposes that this common state will have a strong Orthodox civilizational core and an Orthodox majority of population, a characteristic which does not apply to the E.U. but does apply (to a greater extent) to the Eurasian Economic Union[193] consisting of the member states: Russian Federation, Belarus, Armenia, Kazakhstan, and Kyrgyzstan.

In Conclusion

In conclusion, we can state that the protection and upholding of the person-and-societal-centered dimension within economic policy, through the avoidance of the oppression of the person, as well as the bypassing of the (local, state-based) community, is important for his psychological health and conducive to creativity and productivity in general, which includes economic and business creativity and productivity.

A Person-centered Legislative System

The Inevitable Impersonality of Law

The principle or the rule and supremacy of law is necessary for the imposition and protection of order as well as equality before the law, and is, in this sense, a catalyst for the unity of society as it is directed to fight against injustice. If this is allowed to remain unchecked, it is a recipe for social division, discord, and chaos. In this sense, even if the law is, prima facie, impersonal, this seemingly impersonal feature is conducive to removing discrimination, either real or suspected, and in this way constitutes a factor conducive to social cohesion and strengthening of the person, given that the person is ontologically dependent on social communion (as well as vice versa) in the sense that his personhood is realized and perfected in communion with God and through him with his neighbor.

Thus, despite the law's inevitably impersonal character, it should nevertheless stand for the protection and the upholding of the person—and not for his or her oppression. The fact that laws are passed by the legislature, that is, by representatives of the people and society, is a positive person-centered element and counter-weight to the inevitably impersonal law. However, the fact that the deputies belong to specific ideological parties and are (inevitably) subject to party discipline is a factor tending toward depersonalization.

THE PERSONALIZATION AND COMMUNALIZATION OF PARLIAMENT

Parties are useful and necessary in a democracy for providing platforms for political debate and pursuing political agendas in an organized, institutionalized way. However, if their power remains unchecked they can cause distortions within the democratic system, creating antisocial divisions and emasculating freedom of thought within society through ideological stupefaction, making fools of others and, in essence, depersonalization. We are not proposing the abolition of parties but the circumvention of their role so that from the moment a candidate is elected to parliament, he is obliged to resign from any party post and repudiate party affiliation. He can be a candidate for a party, but if and when he is elected, he must resign in order to emphasize the fact that he now belongs entirely to society and is not subject to party discipline or any logic of balancing between social and party loyalty.

In order to further promote the goal of strengthening the aspect of harmony (within parliament), and weakening impersonal ideologicalization, Members of Parliament should be able to hold their posts "for life" (i.e., up to retirement age to be decided by law) without reelection so that M.P. dependency on parties is not perpetuated through the back door. This "longevity" of the term of an M.P. will force the electorate to think very seriously before electing him. It will force citizens to approach elections with extreme seriousness, knowing that any lightness and recklessness on their part will have serious consequences. In this way, electoral processes will become really crucial as befits a democracy. They will not just be superficially exciting like a football match, but really crucial for the future of the land. The "longevity" of the elected officials will give them the opportunity to concentrate on producing work for the good of the country and not on public relations with the sole aim of winning the next elections. We believe that these advantages outweigh the risk of electing and then not being able to remove an unworthy member (save through impeachment proceeding for specific criminal offences) because the electorate will be fully aware of this risk (of unworthiness) when choosing who is competent and worthy to represent them.

The "longevity" of the elected officials is in line with Orthodox person-centeredness, upholding the integrity of the M.P. and reducing the possibility of him being a straw man and a puppet of hidden political and economic interests. Of course, if he wants, he can become a puppet, but he will not have to do so to ensure his re-election. So the people should and will be encouraged to be vigilant to examine the quality of the character of those they elect. Such a balanced reduction of the influence (but not abolition) of political parties will strengthen the citizen in his effort to develop freedom of thought beyond party fanaticism and ideological hallucinations.

A Person-centered Judicial System

THE RELATIONSHIP OF ROMAN LAW WITH ORTHODOXY

The Christianized Roman Empire, with the capital of New Rome–Constantinople, lasted over 1,000 years until the fall of Constantinople in 1453. The Schism or secession in 1054, of the Patriarchate of Rome from the other four Patriarchates, i.e., that of Constantinople, Alexandria, Antioch, and Jerusalem and the creation of the so-called "Roman Catholic Church," took place more than seven centuries after the transfer of the capital of the Roman Empire from Rome to New Rome–Constantinople (330 AD). Thus, the Patriarchate of Rome was united (in Orthodoxy) with the other four Patriarchates (also based in the Roman Empire) for more than seven centuries after New Rome had become the capital of the Roman Empire by decision of Emperor Constantine. This unity lasted until the Schism of 1054.

On the basis of this, it can be seen that Christianity within the Roman Empire was never centered on Papism (or "Catholic Christianity"), neither before or after the Schism.[194] Before the Schism, the Roman Patriarchate was one of the five ancient Patriarchates based territorially in the Roman Empire. It enjoyed a primacy of honor or seniority, as primus inter pares, and not a primacy of jurisdictional authority over the other Patriarchates. Such primacy, based on both seniority and equality, is in line with the synodic system which is (at least officially) adhered to until today by the other four ancient Orthodox Patriarchates and all other Orthodox local Churches founded in the meantime, which forbids the intervention of one local Orthodox Church into the affairs of another.[195]

Thus, the Roman Pope was an Orthodox Pope until the Schism of 1054.[196] He ceased to be Orthodox (and in fact ceased to be Roman as well) after the Schism when he seceded from the other four Christian Patriarchates which were territorially based in the Christianized Roman Empire. Indeed, after the Schism of 1054, Papism is geographically Roman, but civilizationally and religiously Frankish, as the papal throne had fallen into the hands of the Frankish occupants of western Europe, who were eager to bring about the Schism in order to alienate the western Roman peoples from their eastern brothers.[197]

Hence, Roman Christianity is, in fact, synonymous to Byzantine Christian Orthodoxy. However, the terms "Byzantine" and "Byzantium," are used to a great extent, by Western historians as a metonym and antonym instead of synonym for the Roman Empire[198] when its capital was New Rome (Constantinople), probably intending to create the impression that the Roman Empire, for some inexplicable reason, suddenly ceased to be Roman when the capital was transferred from Rome to New Rome (Constantinople).[199] That is why (just to give one example) the great legal reformer and codifier of the Roman Law, Justinian (who ruled between 527 and 565 AD), is generally referred to as a "Byzantine Emperor" whereas he himself, as well as his nation, would have referred to him as a "Roman Emperor," as the term "Byzantine" is ex post facto and would have been meaningless if used during the said period.

Hence, Roman Law is influenced decisively by Orthodox Christianity for the simple reason that the Roman Empire itself, from the date of the legalization of Christianity in 313 (on the basis of the edict of Milan[200]) until the fall of its capital (New Rome-Constantinople) in 1453, was in fact an Orthodox Christian Empire.

THE SUPERIORITY OF THE COMMON LAW SYSTEM IN TERMS OF THE CENTRALITY OF THE MAN-IN-RELATION TO MAN

We submit that the system of Common Law (a combination of Anglo-Saxon and Roman legal traditions[201]) compared to the continental European system (also greatly influenced by Roman Law[202]) meets to a greater extent the criterion of protecting and upholding the centrality and importance within society of the person-in-relationship to others.

More specifically, we consider that the Common Law system is superior regarding the fair administration of justice, and the *appearance* of fair administration of justice.[203] Needless to say that the degree to which this criterion is met is directly relevant to, and reinforcing of, the unity of society, since any sense of injustice is a factor tending toward disrupting social unity and cohesion.

A key distinguishing feature of the Common Law system is the ability of judges in applying a law to the specific facts of a case, to create, through their judgment, case law or Judge-made law, which a lower court is obliged to follow in dealing with a future case based on substantially indistinguishable facts. The judge in his interpretation or formulation of the law (enacted by parliament, i.e., "statutory law") has some (albeit limited) freedom and power to limit any unjust consequences arising from its application, provided that this freedom is not used arbitrarily but in a way which accords with the intention of the legislator.[204] This interpretation of the law creates a precedent which in itself is a source of law which complements and clarifies the statutory law enacted by Parliament in a way that facilitates its application as fairly as possible. This complementary role of the Judge (to "make law" while at the same time applying it in a case) creates more legal certainty because the citizen can receive legal advice not only based on the statutory law but also on how this law has been applied in practice. Thus the citizen feels greater certainty and familiarity regarding the consequences of law enforcement, thus facilitating efforts aimed at reaching out-of-court settlements.[205]

We believe that the abovementioned feature provides a man-and-harmony-centered counterweight to the (inevitably) impersonal character of the law, a safeguard against legal totalitarianism, and a judicial immersion of laws in a pool of social experience created from previous case law, with the aim, not only of implementing these laws in a given case, but also of adapting and reconciling them with preexisting case-law. In other words, it is a kind of social, communal verification regarding the way a law should be implemented (through the social experience offered by the previous case-law) which acts as a counterweight to the inevitable impersonality of the law.[206] It does indeed seem to be in accord with the saying of Heracletus that "in communion we find truth, whereas in individual privacy we lie."[207] It is also in harmony with the Orthodox tradition where the "Law" is not only based on the Scriptures or the Decisions of the Synods but also on the interpretations of these "Laws" in Christ by the Church Fathers over the centuries. That is, these interpretations act as complementary or explanatory source of law provided that they are based on agreement among the Fathers giving rise to what in Church language is called "Consensus Patrum."[208]

Apart from the quality of case law being a source of law, another distinctive feature of common law is the adversarial justice system. According to this principle, the Judge during the hearing of the case has a role similar to that of a referee in a sports match, i.e., ensures the smooth conduct of the trial by applying rules and laws, but does not intervene in search of the truth himself (as in the continental "inquisitorial" legal system[209]). It lets the two opposing versions of the truth clash and then, taking into account which of the two sides has the burden of proving its case and to what standard (e.g., balance of probabilities or beyond any reasonable doubt), decides whether he has managed to discharge it or not. In this way, the trial unfolds in a lively atmosphere with a dominant role given to oral testimony, which reinforces, through the element of directness, the person-centered parameter. Moreover, the more passive role of the judge

creates more clarity and certainty regarding his role, limiting the proba-
bility of disorienting surprises which would inevitably arise if he had the
privilege of intervening, on his own initiative, in search of the truth in
a case before him.[210] Such an intervention would be completely unpre-
dictable as no one could know in advance the extent or direction or how
objective or biased his intervention would be, increasing the possibility
of creating a sense of injustice to the losing party, which would not only
be directed against the impersonal law, but also to the persons involved in
the trial, and especially to the leading figure who is the judge, thus giving
rise to an antisocial and anti-communal rift and division between judge
and losing party, judicial authority and citizen.[211]

Another key feature of the adversarial system which, although not
absent, it is nonetheless comparatively less pronounced in the continental
system, is the public trial. The public trial typically consists of the examination and cross-examination of witnesses, and is directly related to the
adversarial philosophy of the Common Law. The cross-examination of
a witness is carried out by the lawyer of the other party, which follows
the examination carried by the lawyer of the party which summoned him.
The examination is "friendly," while the cross-examination is confrontational so that the testimony of a witness is effectively tested in order to
maximize the chances of exposing any inconsistencies or lies. This is also
a key element of person-centeredness that contrasts with a more bureaucratic (and impersonal) type of administration of justice that relies more
on the written assertions of the litigants, and where the final decision is
based on processes and persons the litigants do not know and appear to
be covered by a bureaucratic veil.

Relationship between Local Church, State, Nation, and Universal World

Priority of Local State-National Consciousness over "Supra-state" National Consciousness

The Church, as a general principle enshrined in Canon 17 of the Fourth Ecumenical Council and Canon 38 of the Quintesext Ecumenical Council, "covariates" in accord with state jurisdictions. In other words, where state jurisdictions or borders change, local churches are called upon, in principle and on the basis of consensus between those local churches which are affected by the said changes, to adapt to these changes in terms of their jurisdictions.[212] It is thus submitted that, in a similar way, the Orthodox Church should favor the covariation of *nations* in harmony with state jurisdictions, so that "national" state consciousness is created on the basis of state jurisdiction, without necessarily abolishing a preexisting supra-state national consciousness, but taking precedence over it. This is because, as stated earlier, the Church has a local and not a national character, so it encourages the nation to have, in priority, a state (i.e., local) rather than a supra-state national character.[213] Furthermore, the state can intrinsically offer a personal and communal hypostasis (or shape) to an otherwise-impersonal territory, as well as to the nation itself, offering a counterweight to an imaginary ideologicization and idolization of the nation which, if left unchecked, can oppose or undermine the Christian Orthodox worldview based on the communion of persons in Christ, within a local and, at the same time, universal perspective. This universal perspective is achieved through transcending but not necessarily abolishing national divisions; through transcending but *definitely* not bypassing the state, as locality.

Furthermore, the state can offer the appropriate conditions for creating a sense of common fraternal identity among its citizens through the goods it provides (or should provide) without discrimination (i.e., common to all), such as security, education, and health. The common state helps create a brotherly bond among citizens through their interaction with and within the state even if they have a different mother tongue or ethnic origin. This personal-communal dimension to social relations is consistent with the Orthodox approach, and contrasts with the ideological, impersonal, and thus anti-communal and antisocial approach, which could, if left unchecked, acquire the status of supreme ideological "truth," superseding communal truth, and thus create nationalistic, antisocial divisions of such scale and intensity, as to culminate even in violence and civil war.

In line with the above view which regards the state as a catalyst for the creation and experience of interpersonal communion among its citizens (even though they may belong to different national groups), the Church should support as a long-term goal and based on the principle of "covariation," and also under the conditions that will be analyzed later, the granting of autocephaly to each and every local Church with jurisdictional boundaries that coincide with those of the state in which she is based, provided that such a state is not historically baseless, and created for the sole purpose of stirring division and discord within Orthodoxy. In this way, the state, the nation, and the local autocephalous Church will coincide and hopefully coexist harmoniously.[214] Such harmony is conducive to the creation of the appropriate conditions for the development of a loving communion in Christ among a people, in a way that may set an example for other nations, encouraging them either to partake in this state structure or to endeavor to organize their own state accordingly.

But if the creation of a new state is historically anomalous, artificial, and calculated to harm the unity of Orthodoxy, then the Church should not support the establishment of such a state or the granting of an autocephaly to enhance it. This, of course, begs the question: who decides whether such a state (e.g., Ukraine, Belorussia, Northern Macedonia) is artificial? Given that this criterion has a strong subjective element, this could and should be objectified vis-à-vis the granting of Church autocephaly, by introducing a precondition (*inter alia*) that a state must at least be a century old before the submission of an application for autocephaly by the local Church located within it, so as to certify the authenticity and "non-artificiality" of this state.

Coexistence of Local and Universal (Ecumenical) Awareness on an Ecclesiastical and National Level

The Church as the body of Christ, who essentially means and constitutes love in the fullest and deepest sense,[215] should contribute to the unity of the nation not in confrontation with other nations but for the benefit of them, provided that discernment, which is the crown of all virtues, is exercised at all times. If the Church constitutes the universal world in its pre-fall existence, then the local Church must also function as a microcosm of the universe, under the Bishop who is in the form and place of Christ.[216] It must, therefore, promote and uphold a harmonious "cohabitual" balance, both between the local and universal Church, and between national and ecumenical (universal) identity. And this, because the concept of nation is not only a unifying force but also a divisive one. It unites compatriots, but at the same time separates them from foreigners. The unifying element of the nation must, therefore, be preserved and its divisive element put in check, and this goal, on the part of the Church, can be promoted when the local Church views, and encourages the people to view, the nation as a specific place and at the same time as a microcosm of the universal world. The nation should, on the one hand, be subjected and acquire shape, form, status, and identity (hypostasis)[217] from the locality, i.e., the local Church and the State (without necessarily abolishing any "supra-national" national identity but subordinating it to a secondary position) and, on the other, be subjected and acquire shape, form, status, and identity (hypostasis) from the person, i.e., the Prelate Bishop (acting in the form and place of Christ) and the King (if there is one) acting as an imitator of Christ.

This is because the Church has a deeply ingrained local character (geographically) and at the same time personal character (under the one local Bishop)[218] and only through the manifestation and upholding of this two-dimensional character can she succeed in upholding her ecumenical status (as universal Orthodox Church). In other words her universality is dependent on her locality. Inspired by this ecclesiastical cohabitation of local and ecumenical element, the nation should also have a local and personal character based on state identity (provided that this is not an artificial, abortive and moribund state) and, through the manifestation and upholding of this two-dimensional character, seek to acquire transcendentally an ecumenical, multinational and even holy character[219] contributing to world unity in Christ. How? First through viewing the locality as a microcosm of the universal world, and secondly, if this is feasible, through the mutual self-transcendence of states or nations for the purpose of creating a union between them within a commonwealth, confederation, or federation with a unifying element, to the greatest possible extent, not so much any common ethnic origin, but above all the common Christian Orthodox spiritual and civilizational origin. Because Orthodoxy preserves and combines harmoniously the cohabitation of the local and ecumenical element, and preserves the dogmatic truth of the perfect loving unity and communion of persons of the Holy Trinity (subject to the monarchy of the Father) while at the same time aiming to transform and reflect this loving communion into a living experience among its members.

Of course, the Orthodox Church should not hinder or discourage the unification of two Orthodox nations simply because the driving force behind their unification seems to be that of common ethnic origin, but should endeavor, to the best of its ability, to promote the common faith in Christ as the superior driving force, so that Christian Orthodoxy is always above the nation in the conscience and consciousness of the faithful. Such an approach would also serve to ensure the solid fraternal and spiritual basis of inter-national unity in imitation of the unity and equality that exists between the local Orthodox Churches, and likewise minimize the likelihood that the union of some Orthodox nations acquires a confrontational or hostile dimension vis-à-vis other nations (who could also be Orthodox) on the basis of nationalism.

Thus, if Orthodoxy does not have the first say, then the union of some Orthodox nations, driven by nationalism, can at the same time be divisive because Orthodox nations of different ethnic backgrounds are indirectly excluded or repulsed from a possible participation in such a common state. Take, for example, the union of Slavic nations driven by the ideology of Pan-Slavism. What Greek would like to participate in such a development given that it is driven by Pan-Slavism? Of course, this does not mean that any union between Slavic nations is necessarily based on Pan-Slavism. Because if, for example, Belarus unites with Russia, this is not Pan-Slavism but rather an indication that the state of Belarus, which was created after the fall of the USSR, was moribund from the beginning did not have an authentic status and solid historical basis, so its union with Russia is merely a return to a normal historical state of affairs. But if, for example and hypothetically speaking, Serbia, a state with a solid historical basis, chooses to unite with Russia, then the Church must be vigilant so as not to allow the ideology of Pan-Slavism to have the first say in such a union, because, as we have analyzed previously, identification and attachment to ideology have a divisive character, and contradicts the communion of persons as viewed by Orthodoxy. In such a Russia-Serbia union, Orthodoxy should have the first say, so that their union is not accompanied by division and repulsion of other nations, especially Orthodox, from participating in such a common state.

In conclusion: communion of persons in Christ presupposes a common locality or place.[220] Orthodoxy has the recipe to turn the locality into a microcosm of the universal world, ecclesiastically. Consequently, it should try to inspire the state, politically, to seek to transform the country into a microcosm of the universal world, not ideologically (i.e., via right-wing nationalist-imperialist expansionism or left-wing internationalism) but civilizationally and spiritually through Christian Orthodoxy. In other words, universality to be achieved both religiously and nationally, in a spirit of Christian communion, and not in a spirit of ideological massification and division. If global unity, whether religious or national, is attempted by bypassing the person-in-communion in Christ within a common place, it will inevitably be based on an ideological approach. Because if the local, personal, communal aspect is bypassed, then the void will be filled by impersonal ideology, which, as per its (non)-essence, will be "based" on baseless imagination (i.e., lacking in person-based, truth-giving hypostasis) leading to anti-communal divisiveness and sacrificing and subordinating the person to the idea (instead of vice versa).[221]

Among the negative consequences of an ideological approach to ecclesiastical universality, one can identify the undermining and distortion of missionary activity, an activity which Christ commanded His apostles to carry out.[222] In particular, the nationalist Christian Orthodox will not be keen to spread his faith to foreigners, because he will view this as a threat to his sense of superiority, or will be interested in spreading it in order to dominate them in a way that contradicts the Gospel. And the internationalist-ecumenical Christian Orthodox will not be interested in spreading his faith at all because he probably sees Orthodoxy as a folkloric feature for which there is no reason to develop missionary activity, since Orthodoxy can coexist with non-ecclesiastical religions or denominations in a spirit of syncretism. Thus we see that ecumenism, if attempted in a way that bypasses locality and personality, is, in (non)essence, merely an ideology since it advocates a world unity without real communion in Christ which can only take place within his one Church. On the basis of this position, we believe that the inter-Christian and interfaith dialogue should be conducted in a genuinely missionary spirit, bearing in mind that there can be no communion with heresy since heresy (i.e., any faith external to the Orthodox Church) is a delusion and a demonic energy.[223] On the other hand, the goal of missionary activity is communion in Christ, so the Orthodox really seek to remove the obstacle of heresy in order to commune with the (former) heretic, and this can be achieved with love and humility in Christ, and not with the arrogant attitude of the Pharisee.[224]

Church and National Symbols

A local Orthodox Church is associated with the nation (or nations) residing within the territory of the state in which she is located, but at the same time she extends her hand to other nations. The use of national symbols by the Church may unite compatriots, but it can also create a wall separating her from foreigners. It may render the Church "ours—not yours," instead of "ours so that it can become yours as well." It is good and necessary for the Church to be part of national identity, not in order to submit to the nation, but for the purpose of enriching and substantiating it, and giving it an ecumenical (apart from a heavenly and eternal) mission. Bearing in mind this ecumenical perspective, it is perfectly foreseeable that the sight of national symbols in or around a Church may deter instead of attract people of other nationalities who may have otherwise been interested in being baptized Orthodox, feeling that they may not be welcome, or may not feel comfortable within a "national" Church of a foreign nation.

Even worse is the presence of national symbols when, at the same time, they are not state symbols (i.e., local), but have a "supra-state" character, as for example in the case of Cyprus. While the state and ecclesiastical boundaries of the Republic of Cyprus and the Church of Cyprus coincide, nevertheless the vast majority of the churches of Cyprus display in their precinct flags of the Greek nation (in the absence of the flag of Cyprus) thus indirectly giving, in our view, the following message: "The local (Cyprocentric) identification and semanticization of the Church of Cyprus is not sufficient for us, we also need the Greek ("supra-state") national flag to strengthen our (church) identity." The Church of Cyprus, however, bears a local identification as the Church of *Cyprus* and has been enjoying the privilege of autocephaly for 1,600 years.[225] Why then does Cyprus need as a label the national Greek flag, which is much more recent (around two centuries old), to strengthen its identity, given that this identity is already powerful and beyond doubt? The negation of the local character of the Church for the sake of a national one constitutes heresy (of ethnophyletism) according to the Great Local Synod that took place in Constantinople in 1872 in which the Archbishop of Cyprus Sophronios also participated. Of course, we are not claiming that the use of the Greek flag by the churches of Cyprus constitutes heresy. But it is an unnecessary feature which gives the impression of bypassing locality (which is a prerequisite of communion) and moving toward ethnophyletism (which is indicative of ideologicization and, as such, contradicts communion). The display of the Greek flag could be avoided, or at least be displayed along with the flag of the Cypriot state next to it, in order to offer a local ("state-centered") and communal counterweight and "anchor" preventing this movement toward nationalization and ideologicization symbolized and promoted by the use of only the national ("supra-state") flag in the precincts of the parish churches of the Church of Cyprus.

Preference and Support of the Church for the Creation and/ or Strengthening of Multinational Orthodox-Majority States, Upholding Orthodox "Supranational" Identity above National Identity (Whether This Coincides with State Identity or Constitutes "Supra-state" Identity)

In order to maintain the balance and coexistence of the local and ecumenical Orthodox character, it is naturally better for the locality to have a multinational identity like the Christianized Roman Empire (Byzantium), as a microcosm of the universal world.[226] The various Orthodox nations submit (without necessarily being abolished) to the common locality (multinational state) which in a way creates a new common Orthodox national identity.[227]

The Church prays for the "union of all" during Divine Liturgy, and this union could include the union of nations. It goes without saying that, from the point of view of the Church, this union should be in Christ, and in order to be in Christ, it must be within and through His One, Holy, Catholic and Apostolic Church (i.e., the Orthodox Church). In other words, these nations in question should be, broadly speaking, Orthodox. Or at least if this union is not "within the Church" *ab initio*, as, for example, in the case of the accession of an Orthodox-majority nation in a federation whose membership comprises of non-Orthodox-majority nations as well Orthodox-majority ones, there should be at least a strong core of Orthodoxy in this federation, so that there is a realistic prospect of a gradual orthodoxization of non-Orthodox or non-Christian nations within this federation, always of course within the framework of mutual respect for the human rights of the citizens of each and every nation. But if such a prospect does not in fact realistically exist, it would be better for an Orthodox nation to prefer a federation where Orthodox states are the majority, such as the Russian Federation, and strive to achieve the development and aggrandizement of this federal state, through which the aim of baptizing the entire world within the Orthodox Church[228] will be promoted and facilitated.

In this spirit, for an Orthodox nation there should be no distinction between national and ecumenical interest, in the sense that what is good for the nation is good for the world, and what is good for the world is good for the nation. Since the Christianization (within Orthodoxy) of the world is in accordance with God's commandment to his apostles, then it is good for every Orthodox nation to realize and fulfill to the best of its ability its mission of evangelizing non-Orthodox peoples.[229] To do this, a nation must, on the one hand, protect its own constitution and unity in order to spread the Gospel to other nations, and on the other hand, it must prove that it is ready to sacrifice itself for the evangelization of the other nation.[230] To lovingly sacrifice its ego, to become "the other" according to the example of the Gospel and the Holy Trinity. To sacrifice even its national identity (whether state-based identity or supra-state identity) by putting it in second place for the sake of a new common state national identity, which binds together two or more nations with a shared Orthodox civilization. This would be a kind of imitation of the self-emptying of Christ on a national and international level.[231]

In line with the above view, the Church could express its support, as a guideline and in principle, for the creation of a Commonwealth or Confederation or Federation of Orthodox States, without excluding other non-Orthodox nations.[232] For example, the Russian Federation is a multi-civilizational and multi-religious state in which Orthodoxy plays an important role. Non-Orthodox are more likely to become Orthodox (i.e., enter or return to the one Church founded by Christ) if they are inside rather than outside a broadly speaking Christian Orthodox empire. The Church must, therefore, sow the seeds of Orthodox ecumenism on a political level as well, and allow time for any political leadership, to the degree and extent that it is willing to do so, to be inspired by Orthodox ecumen-ism which does not impose an abolition of nations but encourages, in a spirit of freedom, their creative communal coexistence, something which can best be achieved within a common state or commonwealth of states.

"Covariation" with a Constructive and not Negating Effect

If the Church supports national self-transcendence toward the feder-ation or confederation of states, nations, and peoples, within the frame-work of a common Orthodox civilization, then this may give rise to the following question: should the Church, therefore, support the covaria-tion of ecclesiastical administrations in accord with state administrations, even when this covariation may entail abolition? Or rephrasing the ques-tion: since the Church supports the identification of the (local) Church with the State in terms of their territorial jurisdiction, how can it support at the same time the transcendental abolition of these states within the framework of their union and federation with other states? In such a case, should the application of the principle of "covariation" lead to the abo-lition of an autocephalous local Church (in order to unite with another local Church) if the state in which it was located had been "abolished" in pursuit of the creation of a common larger, federal state? And if that were the case, would this not create a disincentive for the Church to support the federation of Orthodox states, if this state transformation would mean the abolition of autocephaly (independence) of a local Church within the framework of "covariation"?

From these questions, it follows that the principle of "covariation" can and should be applied only constructively and not negatively. That is, from the moment autocephaly is given to a local Church then this gift is irrevocable in accordance with the irrevocability of the gifts of the Holy Spirit.[233] This is in line with ecclesiastical tradition and history since all five ancient Patriarchates (Rome, New Rome, Alexandria, Antioch, and Jerusalem) were created within a single state, the Roman Empire, and were certainly not abolished due to the disintegration of this state. There is also not a single case in ecclesiastical history of a formal revocation or abolition of autocephaly. Therefore, there is no dogmatic, ecclesiological or pastoral obstacle to the existence of more than one autocephalous local Church in a single state, as was the case in the Christianized Roman Empire (Byzantium).

Conclusion

In conclusion, we can prioritize the goals or approaches that the Orthodox Church could, or should, have and pursue in terms of the relationship between the local Church, state, nation, and universal world, starting from the most basic level and ending with the most important and final goal, even if this is not immediately applicable and feasible within the present circumstances:

1. The creation of national Orthodox-majority states, each with a local autocephalous Church (provided that these states have a solid historical basis, they are not moribund, divisive creations, and are at least a century old, as a precondition for the submission of an application for autocephaly by the local Church located within it).
2. The creation of various multinational Orthodox-majority states, within the framework of mutual national and state self-transcendence, *without* this transcendence entailing the abolition of the autocephaly (independence) of local Churches located in the formerly independent states.
3. A single universal ecumenical Orthodox (or primarily Orthodox) multinational state, without the abolition of autocephaly of local Churches.
4. A universal ecumenical, multinational Orthodox state that covers the entire planet and all the nations of the earth, without abolishing the autocephaly of local Churches.

The national transcendence should generally be achieved through the medium of Orthodoxy at every stage of the union of states and nations, and not by nationalism. For this reason, it is necessary to prioritize and elevate Orthodoxy above the nation and (additionally and accordingly) prioritize and elevate the state (as well) above the nation (where state and nation do not coincide in the people's consciousness) so that the nation is subject to the state and hypostasized by the state, and so prevented from acquiring uncontrollable ideological power which might allow it to operate antagonistically vis-à-vis Orthodoxy. If, however, the state itself is antagonistic to Orthodoxy, being an artificial and moribund construction calculated to damage Orthodox unity, then such elevation of the state above the nation should not be supported as this would not be conducive to the increase of Orthodox influence.

In conclusion (and subject to the above proviso), the local and state-centered organization of local Orthodox Churches does not contradict Orthodoxy's ecumenical mission, but instead can prove to be a strong basis for achieving its ecumenical goals, free from the burdens and distortions of nationalism.

The Orthodox Diaspora

Definition

The Orthodox diaspora is a phenomenon that appeared in Church history from the nineteenth century and continued into the twentieth. The diaspora, as a religious phenomenon, emerged after the Bolshevik Revolution in 1917 in Russia, and again after the imposition of communist atheist regimes in Orthodox countries of Eastern Europe following World War II. Further waves were generated after the Turkish invasion of Cyprus in 1974, the fall of the Soviet Union in 1991, the accession of countries with large or majority Orthodox populations into the European Union from 1981 onwards and more recently still as a consequence of the civil wars in Lebanon and Syria. These events and other historical, socioeconomic, and political developments created waves of Orthodox immigrants who settled in new homelands, such as Western Europe, the Americas, and Australasia. There, these people created their new homes and their new Churches based on their respective national identity, with the help of which they maintained their ties with their mother Church, their homeland, and their language.

Diaspora and Ecclesiastical Disorder

Despite the understanding that can be shown for the creation of Churches based on national identity under the circumstances previously described, nevertheless the current state of affairs in the diaspora violates the canonical order of the Church, according to which locality takes priority over nationality. More specifically, according to state of affairs within Orthodox diaspora, there are many (more than one) bishops with jurisdiction over the same territory (e.g., U.S.A.) from different ecclesiastical jurisdictions (e.g., Russia, Romania, Bulgaria, Greece), thus undermining the local character of the Church and giving the impression that Church order and organization is based on national (instead of local-territorial) divisions, violating Canon 8 of the First Ecumenical Council of Nicaea (in 325),[234] as well as (indirectly) the Canon of the local Synod of Constantinople (in 1872) condemning ethnophyletism.[235]

The Ecumenical and Missionary Transcendence of Ecclesiastical Disorder

The ecumenical nature of Orthodoxy renders the issue of Orthodox diaspora crucially important. Although the uncanonical expansion of dioceses within the jurisdiction of the Ecumenical Patriarchate may, in part, be based on ethnophyletic motives, the problem could be overcome by utilizing the missionary aspect of this expansionism and, at the same time, checking and controlling the ethnophyletic aspect. In this way the presence of the diaspora could provide an impetus for the implementation of Christ's commandment for the discipleship of all nations.[236]

The Orthodox diaspora could, and indeed should be, the par excellence field of application of a supranational, ecumenical ecclesiastical policy.[237] If the source of evil is the conformation of the Churches of the diaspora with nationality or even worse nationalism, then the problem must be tackled at its root, with the introduction of a drastic measure of "denationalization" and "localization" of these Churches. And the measure proposed is this: the liturgical language of the Churches of the diaspora should be only the local language of the country in which they are hosted in at least 50 percent of their respective parishes (or any other proportion jointly decided by all Orthodox Churches who exercise extra-territorial jurisdiction within a foreign country). That is, the number of Russian-speaking or Greek-speaking or Romanian-speaking parishes in England (for example) to be reduced by 50 percent and the remaining 50 percent to become English-speaking, respectively. This measure aims to drastically expand the use of the local language in official liturgical services irrespective of the mother tongue of the majority of the flock, in accordance with the example of Cyril and Methodius who gave priority to the local, rather than national, character of the Church when converting the Slavs to Christianity. In this way, the local population will not face any language barrier, nor will they feel that by becoming a member of the Orthodox Church they will have to sacrifice their national identity for the sake of another national identity.[238] This measure of linguistic adaptation within local communities may also provide the impetus for a healthy competition between Orthodox Churches from different jurisdictions de facto located (albeit uncanonically) within the same territory: the more local a Church is (e.g., uses the local language) and generally adapted to local customs (without sacrificing Orthodoxy) the greater number of non-Orthodox it will attract. In this way, we believe that Christ's exhortation is followed: "If anyone desires to be first, he shall be last of all and servant of all."[239] as well as Paul's: "I have become all things to all men, that I might by all means save some."[240]

The Principle of "Covariation" and the Orthodox Diaspora

A basic mission of the extraterritorial Churches hosted in foreign countries should be to engage in missionary activity, but also work in the direction of creating the necessary conditions for the establishment of a local autocephalous Church there, within the framework of the principle of "covariation,"[241] with the boundaries of its jurisdiction coinciding with those of the state within which it is and will be located, when the local Orthodox population reaches or exceeds, for example, the proportion of 5 percent of the total local population (or any other proportion that may be decided jointly). In such a case, all the extraterritorial Churches, which happen to be hosted in the same state (uncanonically albeit de facto), must be ready to give their place to the new independent autocephalous local Church, in a spirit of Christ-like humility and self-denial. In this way, we believe that the canonical problem of multiple jurisdictions within one territory can be overcome and even transformed into an advantage.

Alongside the commandment for missionary activity, therefore, the principle of "covariation" should also be implemented, and serve as a source of guidance regarding the Orthodox diaspora and its activities. Based on the principle of "covariation," the following should be recognized as a long-term target: the establishment of a local autocephalous Orthodox Church in every independent state where there is an Orthodox diaspora, with the boundaries of jurisdiction of this local Church coinciding with those of the said independent state. In this way, Orthodoxy will remain and be further reinforced as a "galaxy of local churches,"[242] with the ultimate goal of the discipleship of all nations, and the Orthodoxization in Christ of the entire world.

Orthodoxy and Inter-Orthodox, International Relations

The Geopolitical Division between Orthodox States

The principle of "covariation" constitutes an ecclesiastical rule[243] and, at least prima facie, its application in the case of the establishment of an independent state entails the granting of autocephaly to the local Church which is located there.[244] The issue, however, becomes complicated when a newly established state is, or becomes, a satellite of forces opposing the most powerful Orthodox state in the world (politically, economically, and militarily), which is Russia. Should the Church in such a case lend prestige to this state, establishing there a local autocephalous Church with its limits of jurisdiction coinciding with the borders of this state? The fact that Russia is the strongest, largest, and most populous Orthodox state, as well as the freest from Western geopolitical influence, is beyond doubt and cannot be considered an insignificant detail. If Russia submits or is weakened or defeated by the West, this, from an Orthodox point of view, will certainly have implications of historical, global, and even eternal magnitude. The Church, serving in this life's and world's "battlefield," cannot ignore this reality. She does not have the luxury of ignoring the clear dangers to Orthodoxy (regarding its human and not divine dimension) that will inevitably and obviously arise from a global domination of the (non-Orthodox) West. Nor can she afford to remain unmoved by the miraculous fact that an Orthodox-majority state such as Russia is one of the most powerful in the world, not to mention the prospect of her becoming *the* most powerful in the world if "allowed" by her antagonists to realize her potential in an environment of external and internal peace and stability. This power of Russia could and should be given spiritual dimensions and implications as it remains a state that upholds Orthodoxy as a key feature of its identity. Its power, even in the form of military power and geopolitical gravity, could be considered a divine gift and blessing.[245]

Russia—"Protector of Orthodox Peoples"

Since Russia is the strongest Orthodox state geopolitically, this, in our view, should acquire recognition on an ecclesiastical level, albeit without entailing any disruption of ecclesiastical hierarchy (of seniority) in favor of the Moscow Patriarchate, nor any granting of any "equal honors" vis-à-vis the Ecumenical Patriarchate of Constantinople. Such a course of action is unacceptable due to the thousand-year-old seniority of the Ecumenical Patriarchate vis-à-vis the Moscow Patriarchate.[246] However, Russian geopolitical power could be ecclesiastically recognized through the recognition of Russia (as a state and not as Moscow Patriarchate), by all local Churches, as the "protector of Orthodox peoples." At the same time, the Moscow Patriarchate should remain, and commit itself that it agrees to remain, in the hierarchical position of seniority that she is in today, that is, fifth place.[247] Through this recognition, Russia, as a state, could have a significant advisory and influential role on ecclesiastical decisions with geopolitical implications, without being exposed to the accusation of secular meddling in ecclesiastical matters, since this role will be recognized ecclesiastically. In exercising this role, it should be the duty of Russia and its leadership to stand by and support the institution of the Ecumenical Patriarch of Constantinople, and work together in a spirit of mutual respect, mutual support and solidarity for the unity of Orthodoxy, but also without hesitating to disagree and assume a (counter)balancing role should the Ecumenical Patriarch prove to be vulnerable to pressure from political decision-making centers hostile to Orthodoxy.

In this way, Russia will be encouraged not to question (directly or indirectly) the primacy of the Ecumenical Patriarch because Russia's own geopolitical or "theopolitical" primacy as a "protector of Orthodox peoples" will be derived from and be dependent on her continuous recognition of the Ecumenical Patriarch's primacy.[248] Furthermore, this arrangement would not preclude the possibility of a future identification and coincidence of political and ecclesiastical center in Constantinople (in case Turkey loses its dominion over Constantinople) in a way that secures the presence of the Russian state. That is to say that Constantinople could in the future be the capital not just of a revived Byzantine Empire, but of an incomparably larger empire, which will include both the Russian and Greek world. And indeed, there is no reason why spiritual unity should not be manifested and reflected in state unity, which in fact could be the catalyst for the evangelization in Christian Orthodoxy of the entire world.

The implementation of this proposal (of recognizing the Russian State as "the Protector of Orthodox Peoples") would be, not only a necessary fulfillment of a moral obligation, but an official recognition that Russia is carrying the heavy weight of defending Orthodoxy against the West on a geopolitical level, and also a measure of resetting and restoring relations with the Greek-speaking ecclesiastical world and healing the wound caused by the informal schism created in Orthodoxy in terms of the cessation of communion between the Ecumenical Patriarchate and the Moscow Patriarchate, due to the latter's granting of autocephaly to a new "Church of Ukraine."

The Granting of Autocephaly to a Local Church

Within the framework of the pre-synodic preparation by the Inter-Orthodox Preparatory Commission (which met in November 1993) regarding the Pan-Orthodox Synod of Crete, a text was agreed on the conditions for granting autocephaly to a local Church. According to this text:

a) a request for autocephaly must first be submitted by the subject local Church to her mother-Church, i.e., the Church to which she is subject and belongs.

b) then the mother-Church decides, at her discretion, whether to forward the request to the Ecumenical Patriarchate of Constantinople, and

c) in the case this request is forwarded, the Ecumenical Patriarchate secures pan-Orthodox consent, as a condition for granting the autocephaly.[249]

Eventually, while an agreement was reached on this text, its final adoption as a synodic decision and canon was frustrated due to disagreement as to whose signature would possess the executive capacity to proclaim the autocephaly: that of the Ecumenical Patriarch only (due to his primacy of honor), that of all the local independent Churches (given that their consent for the granting of autocephaly is necessary and reflecting the unity of the universal Orthodox Church), or that of both the Ecumenical Patriarch and the prelate of the mother-Church from which the local Church is seeking autocephalous independence?[250] The fact that this disagreement was so deep as to lead to the collapse of the negotiations to reach a common decision reflects a profound lack of trust between the Ecumenical Patriarchate and the Moscow Patriarchate. From the point of view of the Moscow Patriarchate, their disagreement was probably based on the view that the precondition of joint signature of the mother-Church (from which the new local autocephalous Church would be born) is necessary for the granting of autocephaly, because, otherwise, if the precondition for "consent" of the mother-Church (or of all the local autocephalous Churches) is lacking in clarity or is ill-defined, then, this precondition may be bypassed, resulting in the granting of autocephaly to the "Church of Ukraine" illegitimately or through the back door. On the other hand, another version as to the cause of the dispute is that this reflects an attempt of the Moscow Patriarchate to challenge the primacy of honor of the Ecumenical Patriarchate of Constantinople.[251]

We believe that, since it is common ground that the consent of the mother-Church is required for the granting of autocephaly to a local Church within her jurisdiction, and given that there is also a precondition of forwarding (at her absolute discretion) of the relevant request for autocephaly to the Ecumenical Patriarchate, it would be somewhat unhelpful and unconstructive not to accept, as a consequential precondition, the co-signature of the mother-Church of the relevant document of autocephaly before it enters into force. In this respect, we consider, with due respect, that the argument that such a view calls into question the primacy of the Ecumenical Patriarchate is unfounded, because the Ecumenical Patriarchate's primacy is emphasized and manifested by the fact that her own signature is always a precondition for the granting of autocephaly, while the mother-Church co-signing the document is different depending on which local Church is requesting autocephaly.

A further measure aimed at regulating in general but also preventing the geopolitical abuse of the principle of "covariation" and the right to autocephaly implicitly arising from it could also be achieved by introducing the following condition before autocephaly is granted: a state must demonstrate its stability and its solid historical foundation before autocephaly is granted to a local Church located in it. Among the applicable criteria could be the age of the state: it must have an uninterrupted historical presence of at least a century as a precondition for the submission of an application for autocephaly by the local Church located within it.[252] With this restrictive measure, the "state-centric" criterion of "covariation" is combined with a necessary test of time to prove the authenticity and resilience of the state in question.

In this way, a compensatory and balancing restriction is introduced regarding the possibility of invoking the principle of "covariation" with the aim of declaring autocephaly. Furthermore, the criterion of "covariation" acquires greater substance and depth so that it is not subject to abuse, especially in relation to political aims of forces which oppose Orthodoxy. In conclusion, the principle of "covariation" of ecclesiastical administrations in accord with state administrations is not an absolute rule to be applied indiscriminately in any case of variation of the boundaries of political jurisdiction, but strives at achieving a healthy cohabitation of Church and State with the aim of strengthening both in their respective (and inevitably overlapping) fields of duty. Should this principle lead to internal division within Orthodoxy, then this per se is a strong indication that it has not been applied correctly and in accordance with its spirit and *raison d'etre*.

Transcending the Diarchy between the Greek and Russian World

Proceeding onto the question of internal divisions within Orthodoxy, the most desirable approach to the problem or potential problem of diarchy between the Greek and Russian world within Orthodoxy is to achieve a greater integration between these nations at a state, political, and civilizational level. As for the level of purely state-political integration, this of course is an issue that concerns primarily the political leaders of the two nations who will have to assess the risks that may arise from such a course of action, and elaborate ways to limit or reduce these risks and difficulties. However, the Church can be a source of inspiration for this strategic course of action, even if it is a matter for the political leadership to assess how and to what extent this strategy can be implemented in practice.

In any case, both Greeks and Russians must be prepared to take bold steps in order to achieve a high degree of integration and alliance. Russia should be grateful to the Greek world because it has given her an invaluable gift which is called Orthodoxy, which has always been a key feature of her identity.[253] Likewise, the Greek and the whole Orthodox world should be grateful to Russia because it is the only Orthodox country which is standing up against a particularly aggressive West (as manifested in the West's military campaigns after the collapse of the USSR). Instead of showing gratitude, however, Greece participates in political-military formations such as NATO, whose main goal and *raison d'etre* is confrontation with Russia (and has even sent weapons to Ukraine in "defense" against Russia after the commencement of the War in Ukraine in April 2022[254]). This certainly should not satisfy the Orthodox world, and the Church should express its opposition to this distorted and unfraternal state of affairs. And Russia, on the other hand, if she really wants to be the geopolitical center of Orthodoxy, she should uphold and promote the Greek language making it accessible to its citizens as the language which played a crucial role in the spreading and teaching of Christianity, through the Gospels, the apostolic and patristic texts, through hymnography, hagiography, catechesis, preaching, and generally theology. More specifically, Russia could take measures to promote the Greek language so that it can be elevated to the second most popular language within the Russian Federation.[255] The same measures could also be taken by Greece and Cyprus in terms of the Russian language. Only through constant interaction and energetic confluence at the political, economic, and cultural levels, and on the basis of the common Orthodox civilization, will it be possible to achieve a gradual unification of the two nations, so that in the future they may coexist harmoniously within a common state, or confederation, or commonwealth, in a manner consistent with the supranational unity of the Church.

Conclusions—Proposals

In conclusion, we can summarize the content of this work in the form of codified proposals. The following proposals belong to the author, but I consider that they are inspired, are consistent with, and express Orthodox Theology.

World Unity in Christ

The Church wants to see the world become a paradise even if "we do not have an abiding city, but we are seeking for the coming one." The Church blesses the effort, as far as possible, to make this world a heaven. In trying to make this world a paradise, we do not replace or substitute in our consciousness a worldly paradise for the real eternal one, since we know that Christ's "kingdom is not of this world," but we express our desire to prepare for it, and even experience it from the present life to the best of our ability and endeavor. In order for the world to become a paradise, the world must become Church, and in order for the world to become Church, there must be, or at least we must strive for, world unity in the Orthodox faith. This proposition is in line with the commandment of Christ: "Go therefore and make disciples of all the nations, baptizing them in the name of the Father and of the Son and of the Holy Spirit" (Matt 28:19), as well as with the commandment to "love your enemies" (Matt 5:44). The evangelization of non-Orthodox peoples, inspiring them to enter or return to the one and only Church founded by Christ, is an act of love and fraternization which, at the same time, could be a catalyst for world unity and peace.

This goal may be regarded as the same as was achieved by the early Church with the conversion of Constantine, and expressed by Eusebius in the following passage:

"Thus all men living were free from oppression by the tyrants; and released from their former miseries, they all in their various ways acknowledged as the only true God the Defender of the [pious]. Above all for us who had fixed our hopes on the Christ of God there was unspeakable happiness, and a divine joy blossomed in all hearts as we saw that every place which a little while before had been reduced to dust by the tyrants' wickedness was now, as if from a prolonged and deadly stranglehold, coming back to life; and that cathedrals were again rising from their foundations high into the air, and far surpassing in magnificence those previously destroyed by the enemy.

Emperors too, the most exalted, by a succession of ordinances in favour of the Christians, confirmed still further and more surely the blessings that God showered upon us; and a stream of personal letters from the emperor reached the bishops, accompanied by honours and gifts of money. I shall take the opportunity at the proper place in my account to inscribe in this book as on a sacred tablet these communications, translated from Latin into Greek, in order that all who come after us may bear them in remembrance ...

The next stage was the spectacle prayed and longed for by us all— dedication festivals in the cities and consecrations of the newly built places of worship, convocations of bishops, gatherings of representatives from far distant lands, friendly intercourse between congregation and congregation, unification of the members of Christ's body conjoint in one harmony. In accordance with a prophet's prediction, which mystically signified beforehand what was to be, there came together bone to bone and joint to joint, and all that in riddling oracles the scripture infallibly foretold. There was one power of the divine Spirit coursing through all the members, one soul in them all (Acts 4:32) the same enthusiasm for the faith, one hymn of praise on all their lips. Yes, and our leaders performed ceremonies with full pomp, and ordained priests the sacraments and majestic rites of the Church, here with the singing of psalms and intoning of the prayers given us from God, there with the carrying out of divine and mystical ministrations; while over all were the ineffable symbols of the Saviour's Passion. And together, the people of every age, male and female alike, with all their powers of mind, rejoicing in heart and soul, gave glory through prayers and thanksgiving to the Author of their happiness, God Himself."[256]

Adaptation of the Church to Political and State Conditions in Order to Reinforce Its Spiritual Work and Influence

The Church is in favor of a healthy and harmonious symphony and cooperation between it and the State in order to strengthen the Church in her spiritual work. It supports the adaptation of the Church to the modern world with the ultimate goal of the ecclesiasticalization of the world, and not the secularization of the Church. The Church views as an essential tool of shaping political thought, both for the formation of political institutions and for political decision-making, the Orthodox view of truth, which regards the truth as being, not an idea or ideology, but a person, and this person is Christ. Christ (as God the Logos and Son of God) is in perfect communion of love with the Father and the Holy Spirit, but also desires to be with every human being who truly yearns to commune with Him. Consequently, in imitation of, and inspiration from, this reality, political institutions and decisions should aim to promote and uphold the person-in-communion, considering that the person derives not only utilitarian benefit, but also ontological existence and hypostasis from his relationship and communion with God and fellow man. That is why the Church is in favor of person-centered and (by extension) commune-centered institutions and policies, which promote and uphold the communion of persons, a reality that differs substantially both from individualism and massification, which are in fact two sides of the same antisocial coin.

The Institutionalized Protection and Implementation of Human Rights within a Person-centered and Commune-centered Context

The Church welcomes and supports the protection and further consolidation of human rights, recognizing that state sensitivity to human rights is a prerequisite for progress, cohesion and, ultimately, the very existence of a society. Human rights should be understood and inspired by the Orthodox man-centered tradition. Man is a social being, and therefore the legislator should aim to provide him with such appropriate rights, but also obligations that will help him in his quest for self-realization as a social being. That is, they will help him to live in harmony with his neighbor without this hindering but, on the contrary, facilitating communion with God as well. The legislator should act as a physician knowing that without the cooperation of the patient, he cannot cure him however effective his medicines may be. For this reason, the democratic approach and democratic legitimacy in the legislative process is important, so that the patient's consent is necessary and sought. The Christian legislator does not indiscriminately criminalize every sin in order to force man to become perfect, since coercion and oppression are far from being in accord with the Gospel. On the other hand, he acknowledges and tries to convey to the people the reality that the notion that sin is a right is not a healthy one. In particular, where an existing state of affairs regarding the criminalization, or prohibition, or non-institutionalization of sinful acts is acceptable to the majority of members of society, then the legislature should not overturn this state of affairs by artificially invoking, increasing, and expanding individual human rights. In particular, the Christian legislator is opposed to the ideologicalization of freedom, as well as elevating the distinction between individual and society to the status of doctrine based on the erroneous proposition that everything is allowed for the individual as long as there is no interference with another individual's freedom. Such a concept ignores the Orthodox view of man as a person, and not an individual, who derives existence not autonomously, but from his relationship and communion with God.

In addition to the protection of human rights on a personal level, special attention should be paid to the protection and development of social rights and goods, such as free and high-quality education and health, within a welfare state, as a practical expression of Christian love by the state to its citizens, thus ensuring appropriate conditions for their happiness and prosperity.

Furthermore, the Church supports the universalization and internationalization of human rights and democracy, in the sense that a state should show the same respect and sensitivity to human dignity, human rights, and the rule of law, not only domestically but also internationally in relation to others states and nations, avoiding aggressive and cynical policies, either through military campaigns or by undermining and destabilizing foreign governments.

The Church Should Encourage the Combined Implementation of Ideologies to Strengthen the State and Serve Society

The Church considers democracy to be an important safeguard against tyranny and dictatorship, as well as a guarantor for the application and upholding of human rights.

The monarchy, as an institution that can contribute to the promotion and upholding of the king as a person in perfect harmony with his subjects, and a personification of paternal love and sacrifice in imitation of Christ;

The aristocracy as a motivating force for moral excellence and sacrificial service of the wealthy for the benefit of the people;

Military culture as a means of enforcing discipline in the public service as a counterweight to the possibility of bureaucratic abuse of benefits and privileges provided by the public sector;

Social solidarity, cooperation, and statism in pursuit of commune-centered and man-centered aims, as a catalyst for the unity, equality and cohesion of society, and a guarantor of the welfare state and social rights and goods, such as free and high-level education and health.

Conservatism, as a necessary brake on the ideologicalization and de-socialization of freedom, and a brake on the elevation to the status of doctrine of the distinction between the individual and society, on the basis of which everything is allowed to the individual provided that there is no interference with the freedom of other individuals. The realization of the priority of the person over ideologies gives the power and freedom to man to be the master, and not a slave, of ideologies. It allows him to combine different ideologies harmoniously and to apply them in the service of the person-in-communion. Combining ideologies is a safeguard against totalitarianism, because prioritizing the idea or ideology over the person can lead to tyranny and fascism. The possibility of combining ideas and ideologies and their social adaptation, immersion, and subjection is in line with the principle: "The Sabbath was made for man, and not man for the Sabbath. Therefore, the Son of Man is also Lord of the Sabbath,"[257] as well as with the Pauline words: "bringing every thought into captivity to the obedience of Christ."[258]

The Church—Institutionalized and Official Advisor to the State but without Institutionalized Power

Within the framework of utilizing secular institutions, the participation and adaptation of the Church with state administration aims at facilitating the execution of its spiritual work. This participation should be aimed, on the one hand, at maximizing the influence of the Church on the state and the people and, on the other, at the complete abstention from secular institutionalized power in order to avoid the conformation of the Church with the world, that is, secularization. Therefore, the Church regards as the highest level of constitutional role that she could possibly have, that of the official Advisor to the State, a capacity that could be activated by appointing its own secular representatives in the executive, legislative, and judicial branches of the state, with these executives having a clearly advisory rather than executive role.

The Church Should Encourage Citizens, Politicians, and Political Parties to Resist and Refrain from Identifying with Ideologies

The Church does not conform to any ideology, because for the Church the truth is a Person and not an ideology. Since the Church, on the one hand, is above ideologies, and on the other, is not above the problems faced by the people, some of which fall into the realm of politics, and given that she cannot and should not adopt an apolitical role, the combination of these parameters leads to the emergence of a general principle that the Church is more naturally at ease and more "herself" in political spaces as free as possible from ideological attachment.

Such a preference to non-ideological politics creates better conditions for the formulation of policies and organization of state structures, institutions, and systems in a way that combines the best elements from different ideologies, and generally encourage man to be a master and not a slave of ideology, to avoid identification with, and idolization of, ideology, and its elevation to a status above the motherland and, even worse, above God. The Church encourages, at the same time, the parties to avoid labeling themselves either "right-wing" or "left-wing" in order to polarize, fanaticize, and entrench their followers behind party lines. On the other hand, a party that refuses to call itself either "right-wing" or "left-wing" shows, at least prima facie, a healthy refusal to identify with an impersonal ideology and to use it as a mask, in a way that undermines and hinders the communion of persons, and contradicts the Orthodox person-centered and commune-centered philosophy.

The Church in Support of the Institution of Monarchy within a Democratic Framework

Inspired by the great and central importance attached by Orthodox theology to the view that truth exists in terms of person-in-communion, the Church advocates the creation of person-centered institutions such as the monarchy, with each king being directly elected by the people, being subject to the rule of Law and the Constitution, and allowed to remain in office without requiring any reelection, until the year of his retirement at an age to be determined by law. The king will be a symbol of the unity of the people, will add dignity and grandeur to state institutions, and will be an obstacle to the domination of ideological parties, as well as of powerful economic interests exercising power behind-the-scenes through weak leaders. Such power exercised behind-the-scenes is in essence impersonal and beyond social control and contrary to the orthodox person-centered and commune-centered political philosophy.

The Church in Support of a Centrist, Person-centered Economic Policy Based on a Mixed Economy

In terms of economic policy, the Church supports a mixed economy and the state (social) control of organizations crucial to the production of public goods, state security, and sovereignty. The larger and more important an economic organization, the more desirable state control becomes, to prevent covert and impersonal political power through wealth or through the operation of foreign interests. And this, not out of xenophobia, but because of the impersonal and covert nature of such a power that may lead to covert control of the state (and society) by foreign and socially uncontrollable interests. In the same spirit of subjecting the economy to social control, the Church advocates the adoption of a national currency as a key tool within the sphere of economic policy, unless the adoption of a common (as opposed to national) currency with other states is part of an effort to mutually transcend national independence within the framework of a common multinational state with Orthodox civilization at its core. On the basis of the same rationale of using the economy to strengthen the state as a bearer and manifestation of social unity, the economy should be based on strong domestic foundations in terms of agricultural and industrial production, so that it does not depend on factors, developments, and international crises which are beyond social control. Likewise, free trade must be subject to the needs of the local market in recognition of the fact that, on the one hand, the free market is conducive to strengthening interpersonal ties within the community by helping fulfill its material and psychological needs, and on the other, that interpersonal communion presupposes a common place to which priority must be given in such a way that international trade should serve the purpose of filling the gaps and complementing the local market, and not bypassing and dominating the local market.

Establishment of Advisory Bodies with Eligibility for Membership to Those Who Contribute to the State Treasury over and above Their Tax Obligations

The Church encourages the establishment of state councils within various sectors with advisory powers, and with eligibility for membership granted to those who contribute to the state treasury amounts (to be determined by law) over and above their tax obligations, and who have a clean criminal record. The councils will be chaired by the head of state. This will ensure the presence of incentives, on the one hand, for the production of wealth and, on the other, for contribution to state finances for the purchase of these advisory, high-status posts, so that the state is strengthened, *inter alia*, in its social and charitable work. Participation in these councils will offer some social (aristocratic) recognition and opportunity for professional connections, in a way that is calculated to provide a counterincentive to the desire to participate in Masonic or other similar quasi-religious organizations.

The Creative "Covariation" of the Church with State Administrations, and the Coincidence and Convergence of State, National, and Local Ecclesiastical Jurisdiction, Identity, and Consciousness

The Church, as a general principle enshrined in Canon 17 of the Fourth Ecumenical Council, and Canon 38 of the Quintesext Ecumenical Council, "covariates" in accord with state jurisdictions. In other words, where state jurisdictions or borders change, local churches are called upon, in principle and on the basis of consensus between those local churches which are affected by the said changes, to adapt to these changes in terms of their jurisdictions. On the basis of, and inspired by, the above principle, the Church should favor, in a similar way, that nations covariate alongside state administrations and jurisdictions, thus creating national consciousness based on state jurisdictions, without necessarily abolishing an existing national consciousness, but encouraging the state-centered national consciousness to prevail over any supra-state national consciousness. This is because, on the one hand, the Church has a local and not a national character (thus encouraging the nation to give priority to a local-state national identity rather than a supra-state national identity) and, on the other, the state hypostasizes the locality and the nation in a personal and communal sense, offering a counterweight and antidote to the ideologicalization of the nation, which if left unchecked can oppose and undermine the Orthodox worldview which is based on the community of persons in Christ with both a local and at the same time universal dimension, transcending national divisions. Consequently, the Church should support as a general and long-term goal and under certain conditions, the granting of autocephaly to every local Church located in every state of the world with its boundaries of jurisdiction coinciding with the borders of the state in which it is located. In this way, the state, the nation, and the local autocephalous Church will coexist harmoniously within a common territory. But if the creation of a new state is an artificial and historical anomaly in order to harm the unity among Orthodox peoples, then the Church should not support the establishment of such an artificial state, nor the granting of autocephaly to its local Church, as this would reinforce an anomalous and harmful state of affairs. Such a course of action would be tantamount to a covert conformation of the Church with the world, and, even worse, with centers of power intent on harming the unity of Orthodoxy. To prevent this from happening, the following conditions should be met for the granting of autocephaly:

a) The state in which the local Church is located, and whose territory coincides with its jurisdiction, must be at least a century old before the submission of an application for autocephaly by the local Church located within it, a fact which would constitute evidence of the authenticity and resilience of this state.

b) The local Church itself has requested autocephaly from the mother-Church from which it wants to secede.

c) The mother-Church, if she consents to this request, forward this to the Ecumenical Patriarchate.

d) The Ecumenical Patriarchate seeks to achieve pan-Orthodox consensus on the matter of founding the specific new local Church.

e) Final approval is to be given separately, both by the Ecumenical Patriarch and by the head of the mother-Church, who will jointly co-sign the relevant document of autocephaly.

Along with the above principle of the cohabitation of state, national, and ecclesiastical identity and consciousness, the Church also supports in principle the creation of multinational states on the basis of a common (between the constituent nations) Orthodox civilization, symbolizing a microcosm of the universal world, and expressing the Orthodox view of cohabitation between locality and universal world. This unifying change does not entail the undoing and abolition of any autocephaly already given to a local Church prior to the creation of this multinational state. The principle of "covariation" will have only a creative effect in terms of the creation of an autocephalous Church within an independent state, and not an abolitionist one in case of unification of states to form larger multinational ones.

The national transcendence with the aim of unifying states is best achieved, not through nationalism assuming supra-state dimensions, but through Orthodoxy, which is a master of the art of local and universal cohabitation and is similar to the perfect community of persons in the model of the Holy Trinity. For this reason, it is necessary to elevate Orthodoxy above the nation, and, in pursuit of this objective, the nation should be subject to the state, so that it does not operate antagonistically vis-à-vis Orthodoxy, unless the state itself operates antagonistically vis-à-vis Orthodoxy, being an artificial and moribund creation with a mission to damage Orthodox unity. In conclusion, the strong local and state-centered existence of Orthodoxy does not contradict its ecumenical mission, but, on the contrary, may constitute a strong basis for achieving its ecumenical goals, free from the burdens and distortions of nationalism.

The Creation of Multinational States or Commonwealths, and the Creation of a Common National Awareness Based on Orthodox Civilization

The Church, in principle based on Canon Law, "covariates" along with state administrations and jurisdictions but at the same time supports and encourages that any changes or variations are in line with the plan of divine providence for the evangelization of the universal world. It is, therefore, in favor of the union of states and nations where Orthodoxy will be strengthened in its evangelical and missionary work, and especially where it will provide the civilizational nexus between nations (if they are united within a common state) or between states (if they are cooperating within the framework of a commonwealth or confederation of states) without this union necessarily implying or entailing the exclusion of non-Orthodox nations or states. This union of Orthodox states and nations is not aimed at confrontation with any other state or coalition of states, but is a step toward the peaceful orthodoxization and ecclesiasticalization of the universal world, with full respect for the rights and freedoms of non-Orthodox. It is particularly important that this unification does not have a (potentially divisive and confrontational) ethnophyletic or racial character and, on the basis of this criterion, and for the purpose of excluding any suspicion of Panslavism, the geopolitical union of Greece, Cyprus, and Russia is particularly desirable to ensure the purity and authenticity of national self-transcendence on both sides, for the sake of upholding and glorifying Orthodox civilization.

In the case of a union of Orthodox-majority states that already have respectively local autocephalous Churches, these local Churches will not lose their independence on the basis of the principle of "covariation" or otherwise.

The Orthodox Diaspora Should Become a Field of Healthy Missionary Competition and Transcendence of Nationalism

The Orthodox diaspora, made up of Orthodox people living in non-Orthodox-majority states, should become a field of healthy missionary competition between local Orthodox Churches serving extraterritorially and attending to the needs of these people. This can be achieved, *inter alia*, within the framework of a strict adherence to a rule promoting the expansion of the use of the local official language, i.e., the language of the non-Orthodox hosting state, in the services of the extraterritorial Churches serving within its territory. More specifically, the liturgical language of the extraterritorial Churches of the diaspora should be the local language of the (non-Orthodox) country in which they are hosted, in at least 50 percent of their respective parishes (or in any other proportion to be decided jointly). This measure aims to promote national self-transcendence of the extraterritorial local Churches involved, in an effort to attract the local (non-Orthodox) population to the Orthodox Church. The more an extraterritorial Church of the diaspora transcends its nationalism, the more members it will attract from the local non-Orthodox population. This measure is in harmony with the local and universal character of the Orthodox Church which gives priority to locality over nationality.

The extraterritorial Churches' missionary activity will naturally be conducive to the creation of appropriate conditions for the establishment of a local autocephalous Church, with the boundaries of its jurisdiction coinciding with those of the state in which it is located. These conditions could be regarded as having been met when the local Orthodox population reaches or exceeds 5 percent of the total local population (or some other proportion that may be decided jointly). In such a case, all the extraterritorial Churches hosted within the same country should be ready to give their place to the new local autocephalous Church, in a spirit of Christian humility and self-denial.

The fair and noble competition between extraterritorial Churches for the "fishing of [local] people"[259] within the framework of transcending their nationalism, and their self-denial for the sake of the creation of local autocephalous Churches (one in every non-Orthodox-majority state), is in accord with the Lord's exhortation: "whoever desires to become great among you, let him be your servant."[260]

In this way, the uncanonical element of the simultaneous coexistence of *more than one* extraterritorial local Church being hosted in *only one* non-Orthodox-majority country, will be subjected to a process of gradual elimination through the creation of an autocephalous local Church in every independent state of the world, provided that this state has stood the test of time (i.e., it has completed a century of existence before the submission of an application for autocephaly by the local Church located within it) thus proving the said state's resilience and authenticity.

Official Recognition of the Russian Federation as the Geopolitical Protector of Orthodoxy

Within the framework and/or in extension of the principle of "covariation," the Russian state should be recognized as the most powerful Orthodox state in the world and the "Geopolitical Protector of Orthodoxy." Such a recognition for the Russian state should in no way be interpreted as entailing or implying the granting of primacy or equality of honor to the Moscow Patriarchate vis-à-vis the Ecumenical Patriarchate of Constantinople, or any change within the established hierarchy in seniority of Orthodox, local Churches. However, it should be interpreted as giving to the Russian state the right to speak publicly on ecclesiastical issues of geopolitical importance, without being exposed to the accusation of secular involvement in ecclesiastical matters. The head of the Russian state will be by the side of the Ecumenical Patriarch of Constantinople in these turbulent and dangerous times, and both will operate in a spirit of mutual respect, mutual support, and solidarity for the unity and global expansion of Orthodoxy.

Appendix

The War in Ukraine

1. On February 24, 2022, Russia launched an attack against Ukraine which it named a "Special Operation" with the stated purpose of demilitarizing and de-Nazifying that country, leading to an outcry in the West which responded with massive sanctions including the freezing of $600 billion of Russian Central Bank reserves in Western banks.[261] As a result of this operation, Russia actually became the most sanctioned country in the world, while before the start of the operation it was second only to Iran.[262] The West also provided (since 2014) and continues to provide Ukraine (until today) with massive reinforcements in the form of modern weapons systems, volunteers, mercenaries, military advisors, and military personnel including special forces, and tens of billions of dollars in financial aid[263] thus rendering that country extremely armed and combative.[264]

2. In order for the West to be able to take such measures against Russia, which could be considered as extremely hostile, an important role was and is played by the international Western media, which were and are mobilized to prepare the ground for these measures and any future even more hostile measures, and for justifying them before the Western public, which is and will be called upon to accept financial sacrifices as a result of the unfolding world conflict.

Historical Context

3. It is impossible to understand this conflict without viewing it within its historical context. Indeed, analyzing international politics outside their historical context can easily lead to distortions and may be regarded as a classic propaganda technique.

4. The birth of the Russian Nation dates back to the period from 945 to the end of the first millennium when the Russian Empire (with Kiev as its capital) and its people, due to Byzantine Imperial influence, joined the Christian faith en masse. In this sense, and given that the Christian faith is still a key defining characteristic of the Russian nation, Kiev can be considered the womb and cradle from which the Russian nation was born and raised.[265]

5. The emergence of a Ukrainian national identity dates back to the eighteenth century, which was the period of emergence of the idea of nationalism and

national state at a Pan-European level, and crystallized as a mass social movement by World War I.[266] Taking today's Ukraine borders as a point of reference, the tracing of the emergence of a common national identity presents difficulties because the western territories were historically within the Austro-Hungarian Empire while the eastern territories within the Russian Empire.[267] The geographical, linguistic, and cultural proximity of the eastern (predominantly Orthodox) Ukrainians to the Russians, in connection with the common historical origin first centered on Kiev, and in conjunction with the cohabitation of Russians and Ukrainians within the Russian Empire and the USSR, may reasonably give rise to the view that Orthodox Ukrainians are, to a significant degree, a branch of a single national tree, or at least a nation fraternal to the Russians.[268]

6. The establishment of the Union of Soviet Socialist Republics (USSR) officially took place in 1922 on the basis of an International Founding Agreement between Russia, Belarus, Ukraine, and Transcaucasia (i.e., Georgia, Armenia, Azerbaijan). It was established as a result of the "Russian Revolution" in 1917 while World War I was still in full sway and in which the Russian Empire was a participant. The communists took advantage of the chaos and instability caused by the destructive war, which was further compounded by the abdication of Tsar Nicholas II, as well as the weak legitimacy of Kerensky's Provisional Government, leading to conditions of instability and a power vacuum, which the Bolshevik Party (under Lenin), with the covert aid of Western financial and political circles,[269] took advantage of and seized power, leading to a traumatic civil war within Russia, in which the communists finally prevailed. This "victory" was, however, accompanied by Russia's defeat in the international arena reflected in her absence from the league of the victors of World War I (in which she would, in all likelihood, have participated but for the "Russian Revolution" and the ensuing civil war) and even more clearly reflected by her territorial concessions, as per the Brest Litovsk Treaty in 1918, to Germany which was already beginning to appear irreversibly as the main loser of World War I![270]

7. Amidst the collapse of the Russian Empire and the creation of a new order, and the shifting borders due to World War I, it was only natural that nationalist tendencies among non-Russian ethnicities within the former Russian Empire, including Ukraine, would reemerge with the aim of resisting their integration into the new communist federation of the USSR. This resistance was violently suppressed due to the victory of the Ukrainian communists (with the support of the already communist government of Russia) despite the fact that even among the Ukrainian communists the desire to resist Russification policies was evident, thus persuading Lenin to implement a policy of "Ukrainization" of Ukraine. In result, the USSR recognized Ukraine as a constituent republic of the USSR

(rather than just a province), and generously ceded to her territories which were historically Russian (such as Donetsk) while also taking measures to promote the use of the Ukrainian language.[271] These "gifts," according to Russian President Vladimir Putin, were given in order not to abort the revolutionary project of creating the first Socialist Marxist State in history. Nonetheless, these concessions can also be considered as being, to a significant degree, the root cause of the Ukrainian problem today.[272]

8. During World War II a significant portion of the Ukrainian people sided with Nazi Germany motivated by a mixture of anti-Soviet and anti-Russian feelings or even by traumatic past experiences such as the famine of Holodomor that took place in Ukraine in 1932–1933 under Stalin or from the nationalist desire to establish an independent state. The collaboration of Ukrainian nationalists with neo-Nazis took various forms such as participation in the administration of Nazi-occupied Ukraine or even in genocidal crimes against Jews,[273] as well as crimes against pro-Soviet rebels.[274] Even today the issue of Ukrainian nationalists' cooperation with Nazis continues to divide Ukrainian society. Indicatively, a significant portion considers the theoretician of the nationalist pro-Nazi movement, Stepan Bandera, as a national hero and was officially recognized as such in 2010 (posthumously) by the then President of Ukraine, Viktor Yushchenko, only to have the award canceled the following year by an administrative Court because Bandera was never a citizen of the Ukrainian Soviet Republic.[275] In any case, Ukraine is scattered with monuments of Bandera[276] and there is also a significant neo-Nazi political and paramilitary presence within it, such as the Azov order.[277]

9. As a result of the Soviet victory in World War II, the Ukrainian territory was enlarged even more (within the borders of the USSR) after the conquest of territories from Poland and Romania. In 1954, the cession of Crimea to Soviet Ukraine by Soviet leader, Khrushchev, took place.[278] Due to these events, Ukraine became (on gaining its independence from the USSR in 1991) the largest country in Europe (excluding Russia). However, it is likely that she will lose this status soon as a result of the ongoing war with Russia.

10. In 1985, a reform policy of the USSR began to be implemented with the aim of restructuring the soviet state (Perestroika) which eventually led to its collapse in 1991. As with the collapse of the Russian Empire seventy years earlier, this collapse was accompanied by a (sometimes violent) awakening of nationalist feelings within some non-Russian ethnic groups of the USSR, along with a desire to escape from the Russian sphere of influence.[279] This was also true in the case of Ukraine which declared independence in 1991 (along with Belarus) within the framework of the Belavezha Agreements, as a consequence of which

the USSR was officially dissolved and replaced by a loose confederation named "The Commonwealth of Independent States" (CIS).[280]

11. Another basic parameter which complicates the Ukrainian crisis is its ethnic/cultural composition. In a census carried out in 1991, the ethnic composition of Ukraine in terms of self-identification and self-consciousness of its citizens gave the following results: Ukrainians 77.8 percent, Russians 17.3 percent, with the remaining percentage being shared between other ethnicities such as Belarusians, Tatars, Moldovans and so forth.[281] Regarding religious consciousness, a 2004 census showed the following results: Christian Orthodox 46 percent (either Moscow Patriarchate or Kiev Patriarchate), Unitarians (Papists) 42.5 percent, Latin Papists 2 percent, Muslims 1 percent, Jews 0.5 percent.[282] Based on the above, Ukraine can be characterized as a state divided between Russian and Western influence.[283]

12. A further very important parameter of the crisis is certainly the successive waves of eastward expansion of NATO after, and despite, the end of the Cold War and the collapse of the USSR in 1991: in 1999 there was the accession of the Czech Republic, Hungary, and Poland in NATO; in 2002 President Leonid Kusma announced Ukraine's goal to join NATO; in 2004 Bulgaria, Estonia, Latvia, Lithuania, Romania, Slovakia, and Slovenia joined NATO; in 2005 an intensive dialogue on Ukraine's aspirations to join NATO commenced at an informal meeting of NATO foreign ministers in Lithuania; in 2006 the foreign ministers of NATO member countries announced their decision to engage in intensive dialogue on Georgia's accession to NATO; in 2009 the accession of Albania and Croatia to NATO took place, followed in 2017 by the accession of Montenegro, as well as that of Northern Macedonia in 2020; and finally in 2022 there was the simultaneous submission of membership application by Sweden and Finland.[284]

13. Another key factor that, in addition to the aforementioned, may be regarded as fueling the crisis, is the aggressiveness displayed by NATO after the fall of the USSR when humanity was realistically expecting the beginning of a new era of world peace. Some examples of recent NATO wars aiming at world domination are the following:

1994–1995 in Bosnia—airstrikes against Serbs in Yugoslavia to reverse their victory in the civil war that broke out with the collapse of that country due to Western (especially German)-instigated separatist actions to undermine the dominant role of the Serbs whom they considered as potential allies of Russia due to strong historical and cultural ties between the two nations.[285]

1999 in Yugoslavia—massive US and NATO airstrikes within the framework of "humanitarian intervention" in favor of Albanian-speaking Kosovars seeking full independence from Serbia are carried out.[286]

2001—NATO bombs Afghanistan to crush, as they claimed, the Taliban and al-Qaeda, but their ultimate goal being to establish their presence near the southern border of Russia.[287]

2003—military operations were carried out against Iraq under a false pretext, namely that Saddam Hussein's regime possessed weapons of mass destruction.[288]

2011 in Libya—amidst a Western-instigated civil war, NATO took command of air-operations, and ousted Gaddafi who was assassinated by rebels.[289]

The same year, in Syria, the first clashes between groups armed and trained by the United States and the Syrian government took place with the conflict soon escalating to a full blown civil war with the purpose of destabilizing and overthrowing Assad, with whom Russia is allied politically and militarily.[290]

2014 in Ukraine—a coup by nationalist forces took place and pro-Russian President Yanukovych was ousted. Neo-Nazi paramilitary groups played an important role with the support of both the United States and the European Union in their aggressive determination to prevent Ukraine from following a pro-Russian geopolitical direction.[291]

14. A further important parameter regarding this conflict is the construction by Russia, in cooperation with international companies, of the natural gas pipeline, Nord Stream 2, with the aim of supplying Europe with natural gas directly, and in this way bypassing Ukraine through which passes the "Friendship Pipeline," thus reducing Ukraine's ability and potential to have leverage over Russia, demanding lower prices and threatening to divert for her own use supplies bound for Europe in cases of a breakdown of negotiations.[292] Nord Stream 2 was calculated to operate along with Nord Stream 1 which was already in operation and also bypasses Ukraine. In June 2015, an agreement was signed between Gazprom and major European companies to build Nord Stream 2.[293] On January 31, 2018, the German authorities issued a permit to start the construction of this pipeline which was completed at the end of 2021, but, after completion of construction, the Germans suspended the approval for its operation by decision dated February 22, 2022, in response to Russia's recognition of Donetsk and Luhansk and transferring of troops to these areas.[294] This is a factor that tends to prove that Russia had no incentive to escalate its confrontation with Ukraine thus giving a pretext for the abortion of a project of extreme geopolitical importance for her, while on the contrary, anti-Russian decision-making centers in the West and Ukraine had every incentive to do so for the same reason.[295]

15. After gaining independence in 1991, Ukraine followed a Western-oriented course in the sense that all its leaders (Kravchuk, Kuchma, Yushchenko, Yanukovych, Tymoshenko, Poroshenko, Zelensky) in general and with varying intensity sought close relations, Western integration, and EU membership.

This orientation was contrary to the historic proximity between Russians and Ukrainians but, on the other hand, understandable due to the dramatic collapse of the USSR and the communist experiment, and the ensuing traumatic sociopolitical collapse and humiliation. Nonetheless, this pro-Western drift does not imply hostility of the Ukrainian people toward Russia, nor does it constitute satisfactory evidence that if Ukrainians had the option to choose alternatively (on an "either—or" basis) between further deepening of economic integration with the European Union, or alternatively with the Eurasian Union after Russia's resurgence and improvement in prosperity under Putin, the majority would choose the first and not the latter. This question could have been the subject of a referendum (which never took place) asking whether Ukrainians prefer joining the Eurasian Economic Union (dominated by Russia) or the European Union (dominated by the West).

16. A generally pro-Western approach was also adopted by the (supposedly) pro-Russian Yanukovych, who was overthrown in a coup in 2014 through violent protests (with the participation of neo-Nazi paramilitary groups and incited by the West)[296] due to his change in policy vis-à-vis Russia and the West expressed through his refusal to sign an economic association agreement with the European Union under pressure from Russia which, understandably, as a reaction to Ukrainian's readiness to commit herself irrevocably in favor of a Western orientation, revoked the preferential status that was in force until then for the importation of Ukrainian products.[297] Yanukovych's subsequent change of course toward the Eurasian Union sparked violent protests in Kiev incited by Western actors and with the participation of far-right paramilitary groups in Ukraine. Yanukovych eventually gave in to pressure and fled, seeking asylum in Russia.[298]

17. In response to the coup d'etat against the pro-Russian president, Yanukovych, and in order to secure her interests in the Black Sea, Russia bloodlessly annexed Crimea while pro-Russia Ukrainians took up arms against the government and declared de facto independence in Donetsk and Luhansk rendering large parts of these areas beyond central Kiev control.

18. In an attempt to defuse the crisis, Russia and Ukraine, with the mediation of France and Germany, reached the Minsk (international) Agreements which stipulated, *inter alia*, the following: Immediate ceasefire, withdrawal of heavy weapons by both warring sides, monitoring of the ceasefire by OSCE, the holding of a dialogue on an interim administration in Donetsk and Luhansk according to Ukrainian law, the recognition of special status of these areas by Parliament, the granting of pardon and immunity to participants in hostilities, exchange of prisoners and hostages, humanitarian aid, the resumption of the provision of social welfare goods, the withdrawal of foreign armed forces and mercenaries, and

constitutional reforms which would entail decentralization regarding Donetsk and Luhansk.[299]

19. Unfortunately, the Ukrainian side chose to interpret this Agreement as providing for Ukraine's regaining control of these areas as a precondition to proceeding with elections and constitutional reform, an interpretation they knew would not be acceptable to the other side as it would expose them to the possibility of being ruthlessly deceived.[300]

20. Amidst the deadlock as a result of the non-implementation of the Minsk Agreements, repeated violations of the ceasefire in Ukraine took place. Although it is very difficult to establish and prove who is responsible, the main responsibility cannot but be attached to the Ukraine government, as the side that clearly showed by its overall conduct that it had no intention for a diplomatic solution to the crisis on the basis of the Minsk Agreements, as they insistently refused to implement them (even though they had signed them). Here-below is a list of ceasefire violations reported by the United Nations.

a) Between April 6, 2014, and February 15, 2015, Donetsk region—2,420 dead.[301]
b) Between May 1, 2014, to April 15, 2015, Luhansk region—1,185 dead.[302]
c) Between 2014 and February 2022 (up to the beginning of the invasion of Ukraine), according to Russian sources and the Ukrainian Foreign Minister, Dmitry Kuleba, the number of victims amounted to 14,000, including Ukrainian soldiers.[303]

The overwhelming majority of the victims are civilians who are forced to endure entrapment in conflict zones, living in basements and lacking in drinking water, food, heating, and electricity, as well as torture, abductions, and death.[304]

21. Before the commencement of hostilities, Russian President, Vladimir Putin, had made concerted efforts to reach an understanding with the West regarding Russian concerns about NATO's determination to continue its eastward expansion establishing military presence even in Ukraine, rendering Russia (and especially her capital, Moscow) vulnerable to missile attacks (even nuclear) from Ukraine in the event of a future general conflict between NATO and Russia. In particular, he demanded, on the basis of a detailed document, that NATO commit itself legally that it will not continue this expansion and refrain from installing weapons systems in countries neighboring Russia.[305] NATO defiantly and provocatively ignored Putin's proposals.[306]

22. February 24, 2022, marks the start of Russia's invasion (or special operation) of Ukraine. Russia claimed that the operation was and is necessary and urgent due to a massive buildup of troops and a planned offensive by the Ukrainian side against the Donbass to impose a military solution to the problem of the

self-proclaimed republics, while the Ukrainians deny the accusation.[307] However, on the basis of common sense, and taking all relevant factors into consideration, including the hostility of Ukraine and the United States toward the operation of Nord Stream 2,[308] it follows that the version of the Russians is more believable, since it is consistent with the fact that the Ukrainian side had no intention of implementing the Minsk agreements toward a peaceful settlement of the crisis and also consistent with a clear intention (by Ukraine and Western countries opposing Russia's geopolitical resurgence) to prevent the operation of Nord Stream 2.

23. Military operations continue to this day and it appears that Russia's aims of demilitarizing and controlling Ukraine politically will only be achieved by the capitulation of Ukraine and the installation of a pro-Russian government in Kiev, in accordance and harmony with the historical proximity of the two nations. Given the West's uncompromising determination to prevent such a development (which would most probably be accompanied by the creation of a multipolar global system and balance of power, as opposed to the unipolar, Western-dominated world which has been in force since the collapse of the USSR in 1991) the world is facing the most serious danger it has ever faced—that of annihilation on a massive scale in a nuclear war between NATO and Russia.[309]

Notes

Introduction

1   A subjective observation to an extent, but cited because it has been a source of intense reflection.

2   "The Church [cannot] base herself on any ideology, even a so-called Christian one ... The Church is not a body of Christians but the body of Christ." George Metallenos, *E Ekklesia mesa ston kosmo* (in Greek, trans.: "The Church in the World"). Apostolike Diakonia tes Ekklesias tes Ellados, 1988, p. 12.

3   First president of Cyprus after the declaration of independence in 1960, and leading figure within the non-aligned movement. Widely regarded as a master of a balancing act between his clerical and secular role, as well as balancing between western and eastern (Soviet and communist bloc) influence in pursuit of enhancing the sovereignty and independence of the Republic of Cyprus, in the face of pressure from Western-dominated Greece which played a self-defeating undermining role under the guise of "national center" in alleged (and false) promotion of "Enosis," that is, union of Cyprus with Greece, which was never pursued honestly by the latter, as became evident when it's junta military government carried out a coup against Makarios in 1974 under the banner of "Enosis" thus giving a pretext to Turkey to invade and occupy half of the island (in alleged protection of the Turkish Cypriot community), with Greece refusing to protect Cyprus militarily with the excuse that it was "too far" from Greece geographically. It was close enough for a coup against Makarios but too far for a war with Turkey.

4   John 18:36.

Church and World

5   This term is used to describe the Christian Church in the Nicene-Constantinopolitan Creed formulated at the First Ecumenical Council of Nicaea in 325 and perfected at the Second Ecumenical Council held in Constantinople in 381. "Catholic" is a word derived from Greek and means "Universal." In this context, and from an Orthodox point of view, it does not refer to the so-called "Roman Catholic Church" which

came into existence after the Great Schism of 1054 after her secession from the "One, Holy, Catholic and Apostolic Church," which, from an Orthodox point of view, is none other than the "Orthodox Church."

6   See also: Martin Nodl (2010), "Summary," in Kateřina Horníčková and Michal Šroněk (eds.), *Umění české reformace (1380–1620)* [*The Art of the Bohemian Reformation (1380–1620)*], Praha: Academia, pp. 530–1.

7   Anastasios, Archbishop of Tirana (June 14, 2016), "Epivevlimeni i Agia kai Megali Sinodos" (in Greek, trans.: "It Is Imperative for the Holy and Great Synod to Be Held"), *Kathimerini*, retrieved on August 7, 2021 from: http://www.kathimerini.gr/863672/article/epikairothta/ellada/ar8ro-anastasioy-sthn-k-epivevlhmenh-h-agia-kai-megalh-synodos.

8   Eph 5: 27.

9   See Rom 8:19–22.

10   Nikos Nicolaides, *Themata Paterikis Theologias* (in Greek, trans.: Questions of Patristic Theology), Salonika: Lydia, 2009, p. 198.

11   Anestis Keselopoulos, *Protaseis Poimantikes Theologias* (in Greek, trans.: "Proposals in Pastoral Theology"), Salonika: Pournaras, 2003, p. 91.

12   Matt 28:19.

13   John 15:5: "Without me you can do nothing."

14   John 13:27: As soon as Judas took the bread, "Satan entered him."

15   Rom 5:12: "Therefore, just as through one man sin entered the world, and death through sin, and thus death spread to all men, because all sinned … "

16   1 Cor 12:13: "For by one Spirit we were all baptized into one body— whether Jews or Greeks, whether slaves or free—and have all been made to drink into one Spirit." Although this scripture is referring to the Church, not humanity in general, it may be seen to apply to humanity by analogy given the inextricable ontological relationship between the Church and the created world preceding both the fall and the incarnation of Christ, as seen in Eph 5:25–27, and analyzed above under the header "The Church Is the Pre-fall World."

17   1 Cor 15:45: "So it is written, the first man Adam became a living being. The last Adam became a life-giving spirit," in combination with John 17:21: May they all "be one, as You, Father, are in Me and I am in You; that they also may be one in Us, that the world may believe You sent Me."

18   The Creed according to the First Ecumenical Council of Nicaea in 325.

19   Gal 3:24 (NASB).

20   See Rom 3:20.

21 Rom 5:20: "Moreover the law entered that the offense might abound. But where sin abounded, grace abounded much more ... "

22 See Rom 9:30–32.

23 Rom 3:20 (NASB).

24 Rom 11:11: "Have they stumbled that they should fall? Certainly not! But through their fall, to provoke them to jealousy, salvation has come to the Gentiles."

25 See Rom 11:26.

26 Heb 2:14.

27 Matt 21:31: "Assuredly, I say to you that tax collectors and harlots enter the kingdom of God before you."

28 See Acts 7:53.

29 Matt 22:14.

30 John 18:36.

31 John Romanides, *Dogmatike kai Symvolike Theologia tes Orthodoxou Katholikes Ekklesias* (in Greek, trans.: Dogmatic and Symbolic Theology of the Orthodox Catholic Church), Salonika: Pournaras, vol. I, 4th edn., 1999, p. 149.

32 Gal 3:24: "Therefore the law was our tutor to bring us to Christ, that we might be justified by faith."

33 John Romanides, *Romeosyni* (in Greek, trans.: Romanity), Thessaloniki: Pournaras, 2002.

34 Athanasios, Metropolitan of Limassol (8.4.2014), "E therapia apo tin arrostia tou Farisaismou" (in Greek, trans.: "The Therapy for the Disease of Pharisaism)," *Vima Orthodoxias,* retrieved on August 8, 2021, from: https://www.vimaorthodoxias.gr/eipan/lemesou-athanasios-oi-thriskoi-anthropoi-einai-to-pio-epikindyno-eidos-mesa-stin-ekklisia/

35 Nikolaos Kavasilas, *Peri tes en Christo zoes* (in Greek, trans.: About Life in Christ), Idhiotike, 2012.

36 See Mark 12:30–31.

37 See Rom 13:8–9. Christ is thus not subject to the law, nor is the law equal to him, even if it is his own law. Christ is above the law.

38 Athanasios, Metropolitan of Limassol, *Kardiakos Logos* (in Greek, trans.: Word of the Heart), Holy and Great Monastery of Vatopaidi, 2021, pp. 174–5.

39 Stavros Fotiou, *The Church in the Modern World*, Berkeley: Inter-Orthodox Press, 2004.

40 "The Church ... coexists with the world but does not identify with it ... Her stance vis-à-vis the world is always critical and controlling, but at

the same time loving. That is why when she 'leaves' from the world, she does not do this in hatred. And when she stays in the world, she takes upon herself the world in order to save the world and not to become secularized by the world. For this reason, the Church avoids, on the one hand, Ecclesiological monophysitism (rejection of missionary activity in the world) and ideological Nestorianism (relativization of divine Truth for the sake of the world)." George Metallenos, *Ekklesia kai Politeia sten Orthodoxe Paradose* (in Greek, trans.: Church and State in the Orthodox Tradition), Athens: Armos, 2000, p. 15.

41   Anestis Keselopoulos, *Protaseis Poimantikes Theologias* (in Greek, trans.: Proposals in Pastoral Theology), Salonika: Pournaras, 2003, p. 91.

42   Matt 28:19.

43   See Matt 5:16.

44   " ... God-Logos, with his incarnation does not just improve the existing human society, but recreates the world, remolds man and founds a New Society, a new creation (2 Cor. 5:17)" George Metallenos, *Ekkeisia kai Politeia sten Orthodoxe Paradose* (in Greek, trans.: Church and State in the Orthodox Tradition), Athens: Armos, 2000, p. 18.

45   Justin Popovic, *Man and the God-Man*, Alhambra, CA: Sebastian Press Publishing House, 2008.

46   "But seest Thou these stones in this parched and barren wilderness? Turn them into bread, and mankind will run after Thee like a flock of sheep, grateful and obedient, though forever trembling, lest Thou withdraw Thy hand and deny them Thy bread." Fyodor Dostoyevski, *The Brothers Karamazov* (Ch. 5 "The Grand Inquisitor") (C. Garnett, Trans.). Retrieved on July 12, 2021, from: https://www.mtholyoke.edu/acad/intrel/pol116/grand.htm

47   "The Church cannot seek to create a theocracy, for the theocratic state would transform the Church from a 'community of believers' into a 'community of those obliged to believe.'" Nikolas K. Gvosdev, *Emperors and Elections, Reconciling the Orthodox Tradition with Modern Politics*, New York: Troitsa Books, 2000, p. 40.

48   Luke 16:13: "No one can serve two masters."

49   See Rom 6:4–6.

50   Matt 27:42.

51   See Heb 13:14.

52   Luke 17:21.

53   Gals 2:20.

Church and Nation

54   "A nation is a territory where all the people are led by the same government. The word 'nation' can also refer to a group of people who share a history, traditions, culture and, often, language—even if the group doesn't have a country of its own." National Geographic (not dated), "Nation," retrieved on August 17, 2022, from: https://education.nationalgeographic.org/resource/nation

55   Gen 11:4–9.

56   This term is used to describe the Christian Church in the Nicene-Constantinopolitan Creed formulated at the First Ecumenical Council of Nicaea in 325 and finalized at the Second Ecumenical Council held in Constantinople in 381. "Catholic" is a word derived from Greek and means "Universal." In this context, and from an Orthodox point of view, it does not refer to the so-called "Roman Catholic Church" which came into existence after the Great Schism of 1054 after her secession from the "One, Holy, Catholic and Apostolic Church," which, from an Orthodox point of view, is none other than the "Orthodox Church."

57   See Mark 12:31.

58   See Luke 10:25–37.

59   See Matt 5:44.

60   Matt 28:19.

61   John 13:34.

62   Matt 5:44.

63   Mark 12:31.

64   See Luke 10:25–37.

65   See Matt 15:21–28.

66   See John 4:1–42.

67   Orthodox Wiki (May 15, 2019), *Phyletism*, retrieved on January 26, 2021, from: https://orthodoxwiki.org/Phyletism

68   See John 11:47–50.

69   See John 18:38.

70   See Matt 5:44.

71   "And what is a merciful heart? It is the heart's burning for the sake of the entire creation, for men, for birds, for animals, for demons, and for every created thing … " Isaac of Nineveh, *The Ascetical Homilies.* Holy Transfiguration Monastery, 2011.

72   See Nicholas Goodrick-Clarke, *The Occult Roots of Nazism*, New York, NY: New York University Press.

73   Christos Giannaras, *The Inhumanity of Right* (N. Russell, Trans.), Cambridge: James Clarke Company, 2021.

74   Matt 28:19.

75   See Matt 8:11–12.

76   Luke 2:32.

77   "I have come in My Father's name, and you do not receive Me; if another comes in his own name, him you will receive." John 5:43. "The beast which I saw was like a leopard, his feet were like the feet of a bear, and his mouth like the mouth of a lion. The dragon gave him his power, his throne, and great authority. And I saw one of his heads as if it had been mortally wounded, and his deadly wound was healed. And all the world marveled and followed the beast. So they worshiped the dragon who gave authority to the beast; and they worshiped the beast, saying, 'Who is like the beast? Who is able to make war with him?'" Rev 13:2–4.

78   See John 10:16.

79   See Rom 15:25–27.

80   Acts 2:5. See Acts 2:1–13.

81   Acts 6:1.

82   Christos Economou (not dated). *E symvoli ton Elleniston Christianon ste Diadose tou Evangeliou sta Ethne* (in Greek, trans.: The Contribution of the Hellenistic Christians to the Spread of Christianity to the Nations), retrieved on July 14, 2021, from: http://www.kostasbeys.gr/articles.php?s=3&mid=1096&mnu=1&id=23171

83   See Acts 15:1–32.

84   Matt 23:37.

85   See John 4:5–42.

86   See Matt 15:24–28.

87   See Matt 15:24–28.

88   See Luke 10:25–37.

89   See Matt 8:5–13.

90   See John 4:5–42.

91   See Luke 17:12–16.

92   Matt 8:11–12.

93   Luke 20:15–16.

94   Matt 23:38.

95   See Mark 15:1–15.

96   Matt 22:17–21.

97   John 19:15.

98   Matt 27:25.

99   John 6:15.

100 John 18:36.

101 See Heb 7:15–28.

102 See Matt 16:24–26.

103 "The scribes and the Pharisees sit [on] Moses' seat." Matt 23:2.

104 Gal 3:24.

105 See Eph 2:15.

106 Matt 13:57: "So they were offended at Him. But Jesus said to them, 'A prophet is not without honor except in his own country and in his own house.'"

107 " … In this way, the Church distinguished herself radically, as body of Christ, from Judaism (this was achieved primarily through Apostle Paul) and severed her ties from those following a Judaic way of life, who wanted to subject Christianity to the letter of the law and Judaic formalism, drowning the universality of the Church in Judaic nationalism (phyletism)." G. Metallenos, *Ekklisea kai Politeia sten Orthodoxe Paradose* (in Greek, trans.: "Church and State in the Orthodox Tradition"), Athens: Armos, 2000, p. 14.

108 See Matt 28:18.

109 See Rom 6:3–5.

110 See Acts 22:25–28.

111 See Rom 11:11 and Rom 11:25–26.

112 Gal 3:28.

113 1 Cor 9:19–23.

114 See John 14:6.

115 Steven Runciman, *The Byzantine Theocracy*, Cambridge, UK: Cambridge University Press, 1977.

116 "In place of Rome which had conquered and subjugated, there appeared a state in which citizens [regardless of nationality] had equal rights, a state held together by the institution of a common faith, Christianity." Stavros Fotiou, *The Church in the Modern World*, Berkeley: Inter-Orthodox Press, 2004, p. 37.

117 Ierotheos Vlachos (Metropolitan of Nafpaktos), *The Person in the Orthodox Tradition*, Birth of the Theotokos Monastery, 1999.

118 John Romanides, *Romeosyne* (in Greek, trans.: Romanity), Thessaloniki: Pournaras, 2002, p. 310.

119 Gal 3:24.

120 See Matt 5:17.

121 Mark 2:22.

122 "The Pentecost led the way to universal and spiritual unity. The transcendence of all divisions (national, class, political) on the basis of equality and unity in Christ of all people." George Metallenos (2008), "Orthodoxe Oikoumenikoteta kai Pagkosmiopoiese" (in Greek, trans.: "Orthodox Universality and Globalization"), *E Alle Opsis*, retrieved on August 15, 2021, from: https://alopsis.gr/ορθόδοξη-οικουμενικότητα-και-παγκοσ/.

123 John 12:24: "Most assuredly, I say to you, unless a grain of wheat falls into the ground and dies, it remains alone; but if it dies, it produces much grain." National transcendence, in this respect, could be regarded as a creative and fruit-bearing death.

124 See Mark 9:35.

125 See 1 Cor 4:20.

126 See Matt 5:44.

127 John 18:8.

128 Jehovah's Witnesses (not dated), *Why Don't Jehovah's Witnesses Go to War?* retrieved on July 16, 2021, from: https://www.jw.org/en/jehovahs-witnesses/faq/why-dont-jw-go-to-war/

129 Alexander Schmemann, *The Mission of Orthodoxy*, Ben Lomond, CA: Conciliar Press, 1994.

130 Gal 6:12–13.

Church and State

131 See John 18:36.

132 "A nation is a territory where all the people are led by the same government. The word 'nation' can also refer to a group of people who share a history, traditions, culture and, often, language—even if the group doesn't have a country of its own." National Geographic (not dated). "Nation," retrieved on August 17, 2022, from: https://education.nationalgeographic.org/resource/nation

133 "The existence of political authority-service is from a Christian point of view necessary for ensuring social harmony, after its subjugation to the reality of the fall and sin." George Metallenos, *Ekklesia kai Politeia sten Orthodoxe Paradose* (in Greek, trans.: "Church and State in the Orthodox Tradition"), Athens: Armos, 2000, p. 56.

134 See Rom 12:15.

135 Acts 5:29: "We ought to obey God rather than men."

136 See Ephesians 6:4

137 Matt 7:6: "Do not give what is holy to the dogs; nor cast your pearls before swine, lest they trample them under their feet, and turn and tear you in pieces."

138 John 18:36.

139 See John 6:15.

140 See Mark 5:21–24.

141 See Acts 25:10–12.

142 "It is typical that in the texts of the Roman/ Byzantine period there is no mention of a relationship between 'Church and State' but of 'King and Priesthood/ Prelacy.' In other words, they are two kinds of service, the political and the priestly/ spiritual one, which coexist and co-serve within the one Body, Gods People, which is at the same time People of the Church … and of the State." George Metallenos, *Ekklisea kai Politeia sten Orthodoxe Paradose* (in Greek, trans.: "Church and State in the Orthodox Tradition"), Athens: Armos, 2000, p. 55.

143 Tomasz Kuprjanowicz, "Tsar Nicholas II-Heroism and Martyrdom," *Elpis*, vol. 21, 2019, pp. 21–5.

144 Canon 7 of the Fourth Ecumenical Council of 451.

145 "'Therefore, the Church does not seek to take for itself the role of government, but stands as a witness to advise and counsel society.'" Nikolas K. Gvosdev, *Emperors and Elections, Reconciling the Orthodox Tradition with Modern Politics*, New York: Troitsa Books, 2000, p. 41.

146 John Konidaris, *Egheiridio Ekklesiastikou Dikaiou* (in Greek, trans.: "Manual of Ecclesiastical Law"), Athens: Sakkoula 2000, p. 71.

147 John Konidaris, *Egheiridio Ekklesiastikou Dikaiou* (in Greek, trans.: "Manual of Ecclesiastical Law"), Athens: Sakkoula 2000, p. 71.

148 Art. 1 para. 4 of Law 580/1977 of the Republic of Greece.

149 John Konidaris, *Egheiridio Ekklesiastikou Dikaiou* (in Greek, trans.: "Manual of Ecclesiastical Law"), Athens: Sakkoula 2000, p. 71.

150 Art. 110 of the Constitution of the Republic of Cyprus.

151 "The idea of 'separation' of Church–State, that is the termination of all (constitutionally guaranteed) cooperation between these two fields and the de-Orthodoxization of the State is clearly 'European' and is in accord with our wider national reorientation in accordance with the demands of our 'Universal Metropolis' since the nineteenth century, in Europe. A clearly European invention is also the concept of 'irreligious state,' the state, that is, which is not influenced in its functions and aims

by any religion." George Metallenos, *Ekklesia kai Politeia sten Orthodoxe Paradose* (in Greek, trans.: "Church and State in the Orthodox Tradition"), Athens: Armos, 2000, p. 58.

152 See John 14:6.

153 Nikolas K. Gvosdev, *Emperors and Elections, Reconciling the Orthodox Tradition with Modern Politics*, New York: Troitsa Books, 2000, p. 42.

154 John Chrysostom, *On the Priesthood, Ascetic Treatises, Select Homilies and Letters, in Nicene and Post-Nicene Fathers* (volume IX). First Series, ed. Philip Schaff, Peabody, MA: Hendrickson Publishers, 1994, pp. 381–2.

155 See 1 John 4:18.

156 Christos Yannaras, *The Inhumanity of Right* (N. Russell, Trans.), Cambridge: James Clarke Company, 2021.

157 See Nikolas K. Gvosdev, *Emperors and Elections, Reconciling the Orthodox Tradition with Modern Politics*, New York: Troitsa Books, 2000, pp. 99–102, regarding the implementation by the Church throughout its history of democratic principles regarding its functions.

158 Christos Yannaras, *The Inhumanity of Right* (N. Russell, Trans.), Cambridge: James Clarke Company, 2021.

159 "'Not all the water in the rough rude sea can wash the balm off from an anointed king.'" William Shakespeare, (not dated), *Richard II*. Act 3, Scene 2, Verse 54–55. Retrieved on July 18, 2021, from: https://www.sparknotes.com/nofear/shakespeare/richardii/page_118/

160 Christos Yannaras, *E Eleftheria tou Ethous* (in Greek, trans.: The Freedom of Morals), Athens, Greece: Ikaros, 2011.

161 "The bishop, as head of the priesthood, as well as the emperor, as head of political service, are 'living images' of Christ. The King partakes by grace of the Kingdom of God and (should) be an image of Christ." George Metallenos, *Ekklesia kai Politeia sten Orthodoxe Paradose* (in Greek, trans.: "Church and State in the Orthodox Tradition"), Athens: Armos, 2000, p. 32.

162 "If anyone desires to be first, he shall be last of all and servant of all." Mark 9:35.

163 Col 2:10.

164 "For where two or three gather in my name, there am I with them." Matt 18:20.

165 Ierotheos Vlachos (Metropolitan of Nafpaktos), *The Person in the Orthodox Tradition*, Levadia, Greece: Birth of the Theotokos Monastery, 1999.

166 Sophrony Sakharov, *St. Silouan the Athonite*, Crestwood, NY: St. Vladimir's Seminary Press, 1999.

167 "Καθ᾽ ὅ,τι ἂν κοινωνήσωμεν, ἀληθεύομεν, ἃ δε ἂν ἰδιάσωμεν, ψευδόμεθα." Heracletus (trans.: "in communion we find truth, whereas in individual privacy we lie." Diels/ Kranz, Fragmente der Vorsokratiker, vol. I, 148, pp. 29–30.

168 "Ideology is a specious way of relating to the world. It offers human beings the illusion of an identity, of dignity, and of morality while making it easier for them to part with them. As the repository of something suprapersonal and objective, it enables people to deceive their conscience and conceal their true position and their inglorious modus vivendi, both from the world and from themselves ... It is a veil behind which human beings can hide their own fallen existence, their trivialization, and their adaptation to the status quo.'" Vaclav Havel, "The Power of the Powerless" (October 1978). *International Journal of Politics* (1979) pdf in website "'ICNC, International Center on Nonviolent Conflict,'" p. 7, retrieved from: https://www.nonviolent-conflict.org/resource/the-power-of-the-powerless/.

169 Stavros Fotiou, *The Church in the Modern World*, Berkeley: Inter-Orthodox Press, 2004, p. 10.

170 Christos Giannaras, *Person and Eros*, Brookline, MA: Holy Cross Orthodox Press, 2008.

171 "Καθ᾽ ὅ,τι ἂν κοινωνήσωμεν, ἀληθεύομεν, ἃ δε ἂν ἰδιάσωμεν, ψευδόμεθα." Heracletus (trans.: "in communion we find truth, whereas in individual privateness we lie." Diels/ Kranz, Fragmente der Vorsokratiker, vol. I, 148, pp. 29–30.

172 "Καθ᾽ ὅ,τι ἂν κοινωνήσωμεν, ἀληθεύομεν, ἃ δε ἂν ἰδιάσωμεν, ψευδόμεθα." Heracletus (trans.: "in communion we find truth, whereas in individual privateness we lie." Diels/ Kranz, Fragmente der Vorsokratiker, vol. I, 148, pp. 29–30.

173 Lenin could be regarded as an example of an ideologue in the inhuman sense. "For mankind at large Lenin had nothing but scorn: the documents confirm Gorky's assertion that individual human beings held for Lenin 'almost no interest' and that he treated the working class much as a metalworker treated iron ore." Richard Pipes, *The Unknown Lenin*, New Haven and London: Yale University Press, 1999, p. 10.

174 Luke 16:13.

175 1 Cor 9:22.

176 "… The Church is body of Christ, that is a society (a Divine-Human Organization) and since it includes people who live in the world … it is not possible for her to be indifferent to 'political service' or to the people who undertake to exercise it." George Metallenos, *Ekklesia kai Politeia sten Orthodoxe Paradose* (in Greek, trans.: "Church and State in the Orthodox Tradition"), Athens: Armos, 2000, p. 18.

177 "Then God said [i.e., the Holy Trinity], 'Let Us make man in Our image, according to Our likeness.'" Gen 1:26. Demetris Kitsikis, *"E trite ideologia kai e Ordodoxia"* (in Greek, trans.: "The Third Ideology and Orthodoxy"), Athens: Estia, 1998, p. 131.

178 See 1 Cor 12:12 in combination with Christ's teaching "Love your neighbor as yourself" (Matt 22:39). If interpreted and applied perfectly this teaching calls upon us to realize that our neighbor *is our self* without either us or the neighbor losing our identity and otherness.

179 "The Communists disdain to conceal their views and aims. They openly declare that their ends can be attained only by the forcible overthrow of all existing social conditions." Karl Marx and Friedrich Engels (1872), *The Manifesto of the Communist Party*, "Chapter IV. Position of the Communists in Relation to the Various Existing Opposition Parties," retrieved on July 26, 2021, from: https://www.marxists.org/archive/marx/works/1848/communist-manifesto/ch04.htm

180 "'In answer to all reproaches and accusations of terror, dictatorship and civil war, we say: yes, we have openly proclaimed what no other government would ever proclaim: we are the first government in the world which openly speaks of civil war; yes, we started and continue to wage war against the exploiters.'" Vladimir I. Lenin in *PSS* (Polnoe sobranie sochinenii) vol. 12, p. 157.

181 "'It is necessary secretly—and urgently—to prepare the terror.'" V. I. Lenin in *The Unknown Lenin*, edited by Richard Pipes. Yale University Press 1999, Document 28, pp. 56–7.

182 Democracy in the Orthodox Church is manifested in the synodic system, See, for example, art. 5(2) of the Charter of the Orthodox Church of Cyprus.

183 "If someone says, 'I love God,' and hates his brother, he is a liar; for he who does not love his brother whom he has seen, how can he love God whom he has not seen?" 1 John 4:20.

184 "He who has two tunics, let him give to him who has none; and he who has food, let him do likewise." Luke 3:11.

185 "'Orthodox values do not preach the forcible confiscation of wealth, but instead encourage the promotion of an attitude where the wealthy recognise their obligations to the community.'" Nikolas K. Gvosdev, *Emperors and Elections, Reconciling the Orthodox Tradition with Modern Politics*, New York: Troitsa Books, 2000, p. 125.

186 Richard Wolff, *Democracy at Work: A Cure for Capitalism*, Chicago: Haymarket Books, 2012.

187 Christos Giannaras, *The Inhumanity of Right* (N. Russell, Trans.), Cambridge: James Clarke Company, 2021.

188 Michel Aglietta, *A Theory of Capitalist Regulation*, New York: Verso Books, 2001.

189 Hasaan Khawar (September 7, 2021). What Can Civil Service Learn from Military? *The Express Tribune*, retrieved on August 19, 2022, from: https://tribune.com.pk/story/2318863/what-can-civil-service-learn-from-military

190 Richard Wolff, *Democracy at Work: A Cure for Capitalism*, Chicago: Haymarket Books, 2012.

191 Piotr Grzebyk, "Legal position of trade unions in Polish Collective Labour Law: enterprise-based trade union," *Hungarian Labour Law E-Journal*, retrieved on July 28, 2021, from: http://hllj.hu/letolt/2014_1_a/05.pdf

192 Benes, J, et al. (2008), *Exchange Rate Management and Inflation Targeting: Modeling the Exchange Rate in Reduced-Form New Keynesian Models*, Czech Journal of Economics and Finance, vol. 58, nos. 3–4.

193 "The Eurasian Economic Union is an international organization for regional economic integration. It has international legal personality and is established by the Treaty on the Eurasian Economic Union. The EAEU provides for free movement of goods, services, capital and labor, pursues coordinated, harmonized and single policy in the sectors determined by the Treaty and international agreements within the Union. The Union is being created to comprehensively upgrade, raise the competitiveness of and cooperation between the national economies, and to promote stable development in order to raise the living standards of the nations of the Member-States." EAEU, Eurasian Economic Union official website. Retrieved on August 21, 2022, from: http://www.eaeunion.org/?lang=en#about-info

194 John Romanides, *Franks, Romans, Feudalism and Doctrine*, Brookline, MA: Holy Cross Orthodox Press, 1981.

195 Ioannis Karmires, *Ta dogmatika kai Symvolika Mnemeia tes Orthodoxou Katholikes Ekklesias*, vol. II, Athens, 1953.

196 John Romanides, *Romeosyne* (in Greek, trans.: Romanity), Thessaloniki: Pournaras, 2002.

197 John Romanides, *Romeosyne* (in Greek, trans.: Romanity), Thessaloniki: Pournaras, 2002.

198 There is evidence of synonymic use of Byzantine to identify eastern Romans as opposed to western Romans during the period when the Roman Empire (with Constantinople as its capital) extended throughout the European continent: Panagiotis Theodoropoulos, "Did the Byzantines Call Themselves Byzantines? Elements of Eastern Roman Identity in the Imperial Discourse of the Seventh Century," *Byzantine and Modern Greek Studies*, vol. 45, no. 1, 2021, pp. 25–41, retrieved on September 2, 2022, from: https://www.cambridge. org/core/journals/byzantine-and-modern-greek-studies/article/ did-the-byzantines-call-themselves-byzantines-elements-of- eastern-roman-identity-in-the-imperial-discourse-of-the-seventh- century/65B940757F334DC5D5F0E6B479045BDD

199 Christos Yannaras, *Orthodoxia kai Dyse ste neotere Ellada* (in Greek, trans.: Orthodoxy and West in Modern Greece), Athens: Domos, 2006.

200 In Latin: Edictum Mediolanense.

201 Edward D. Re, *The Roman Contribution to the Common Law*. 29 Fordham L. Rev. 447 (1961), retrieved on August 20, 2021, from: https:// ir.lawnet.fordham.edu/flr/vol29/iss3/2

202 Patrick Glenn, *Legal Traditions of the World*, 4th edn., Oxford: Oxford University Press, 2010, p. 140.

203 See Patrick Devlin, *The Judge*, Oxford: Oxford University Press, 1979, p. 3.

204 Patrick Devlin, *The Judge*, Oxford: Oxford University Press, 1979, p. 14.

205 Patrick Devlin, *The Judge*, Oxford: Oxford University Press, 1979, pp. 179–81.

206 Patrick Glenn, *Legal Traditions of the World*, 4th edn., Oxford: Oxford University Press, 2010, pp. 247–53.

207 "Καθ᾽ ὅ,τι ἂν κοινωνήσωμεν, ἀληθεύομεν, ἃ δε ἂν ἰδιάσωμεν, ψευδόμεθα." Diels/ Kranz, Fragmente der Vorsokratiker, vol. I, 148, pp. 29–30.

208 Yulia Rozumna and Mina Soliman (2018), "The Consensus Patrum: What Is It?" *Orthodoxy in Dialogue*, retrieved on July 30, 2021, from: https://orthodoxyindialogue.com/2018/01/06/the-consensus- patrum-what-is-it-by-yulia-rozumna-and-mina-soliman/

209 Patrick Glenn, *Legal Traditions of the World*, 4th edn., Oxford: Oxford University Press, 2010, p. 144.

210 Patrick Glenn, *Legal Traditions of the World*, 4th edn., Oxford: Oxford University Press, 2010, p. 257.

211 "'In the course of their work judges quite often dissociate themselves from the law. They would like to decide otherwise, they hint, but the law does not permit. They emphasize that it is as binding upon them as it is upon the litigants. If a judge leaves the law and makes his own decisions, even if in substance they are just, he loses the protection of the law and sacrifices the appearance of impartiality which is given by adherence to the law ... But if the stroke is inflicted by the law, it leaves no sense of individual injustice; the losing party is not a victim who has been singled out; it is the same for everybody, he says. And how many a defeated litigant has salved his wounds with the thought that the law is an ass!'" P. Devlin, *The Judge*, Oxford: Oxford University Press, 1979, p. 4.

Relationship between Local Church, State, Nation, and Universal World

212 " ... if by the command of the Emperor a city be renewed, the order of ecclesiastical parishes shall follow the civil and public forms." Canon 17 of the Fourth Ecumenical Council.
     "If any city be renewed by imperial authority, or shall have been renewed, let the order of things ecclesiastical follow the civil and public models." Canon 38 of Quintesext Ecumenical Council.

213 For example, first Australian then Anglo-Saxon, first Egyptian then Arab, first Cypriot then Greek.

214 "In the East, however, Christianity, in its worldly dimension, was transformed into a state religion ... while in the West it was reduced to an individual religion ... " George Metallenos (2006), "Orthodoxia kai Fanatismos" (in Greek, trans.: "Orthodoxy and Fanaticism"), *E Alle Opsis*, retrieved on August 15, 2021, from: https://alopsis. gr/%ce%bf%cf%81%ce%b8%ce%bf%ce%b4%ce%bf%ce%be%ce% af%ce%b1-%ce%ba%ce%b1%ce%b9-%cf%86%ce%b1%ce%bd%c e%b1%cf%84%ce%b9%cf%83%ce%bc%cf%8c%cf%82-%cf%80%- cf%81%cf%89%cf%84%ce%bf%cf%80%cf%81%ce%b5%cf%83%ce%b2/

215 1 John 4:16.

216 "Wherever the bishop shall appear, there let the multitude of the people also be; even as, wherever Jesus Christ is, there is the Catholic

Church." Epistle of Ignatius to the Smyrnaeans, *New Advent*, Chapter 8. Retrieved on September 1, 2021, from: https://www.newadvent.org/fathers/0109.htm (N.B. the term "Catholic" means "Universal" and not the Church under the Pope, as this epistle was written around the year 110, more than nine centuries before the Schism).

217   "Hypostasis" as in the fullest and most authentic form of existence a nation can possibly achieve in imitation (however imperfect) of Christ.

218   "For in one church there shall not be two bishops." Canon 8 of the First Ecumenical Council of Nicaea.

219   In other words, achieve the fullest and most authentic form of existence a nation can possibly achieve in imitation (however imperfect) of Christ. See Matt 25:32 indicating that there is an eternal dimension to nations: "All the nations will be gathered before Him, and He will separate them one from another, as a shepherd divides his sheep from the goats." And 1 Pet 2:9–10: "But you are a chosen people, a royal priesthood, **a holy nation**, His own special people, that you may proclaim the praises of Him who called you out of darkness into His marvelous light; who once *were* not a people but *are* now the people of God" (my emphasis).

220   Christos Yannaras, *The Inhumanity of Right* (N. Russell, Trans.), Cambridge: James Clarke Company, 2021.

221   Imagination is a spiritual disease causing "diseases such as religion, racism, nationalism, sexual perversion, greed, gluttony etc. … [and can be] cured by the two kinds of prayer: the one is centers in the brain and is performed at certain moments, and [the other] is the incessant prayer of the heart … " John Romanides, *Romeosyni* (in Greek, trans.: Romanity), Thessaloniki: Pournaras, 2002, pp. 58–9.

222   See Matt 28:19.

223   Epiphanius, *Panarion 69,2*, PG 42, 2014 AB.

224   See Luke 18:9–14.

225   On the basis of Canon 8 of the Third Ecumenical Council of Ephesus in 431.

226   "The unification of the known world into an *oikoumene* (world) had first been achieved by Alexander the Great who went beyond the borders of the nations of his time and created a unity that guaranteed a common framework of life. The Roman Empire was the second realization of the *oikoumene*. This was not a single state, but a single order of things, the *Pax Romana*, and it ensured a peaceful co-existence of people and nations on the basis of the Roman Law. When Constantine transferred the capital of the state from Rome to Constantinople, he laid the

foundations for the third *oikoumene*. In place of Rome, which had conquered and subjugated, there appeared a state in which citizens had equal rights, a state held together by the institution of a common faith, Christianity." Stavros Fotiou, *The Church in the Modern World*, Berkeley: Inter-Orthodox Press, 2004, pp. 36–7.

227 George Mantzarides, Orthodoxi Theologia kai Koinoniki Zoe (in Greek, trans.: Orthodox Theology and Social Life), Salonika: Pournara, 1996, p. 182.

228 See also Alexander Yanov, *The Russian Challenge and the Year 2000*, New Jersey: Wiley–Blackwell 1987, p. 236, quoting G.M. Shimanov regarding the view of the internal transformation of the USSR into an orthodox-oriented state with a mission to "orthodoxize" the entire world.

229 This sense of mission is evident in Dostoyevsky regarding the Russian nation: "To be a true Russian does indeed mean to aspire finally to reconcile the contradictions of Europe, to show the end of European yearning in our Russian soul, omnihuman and all uniting, to include within our soul by brotherly love all our brethren, and at last, it may be, to pronounce the final Word of the great general harmony, of the final brotherly communion of all nations in accordance with the Law of the Gospel of Christ!" Fyodor Dostoyevski, *Celebration of Pushkin's Birth, June 8 1880*, retrieved on August 9, 2021, from: http://www.speeches-usa.com/Transcripts/feyodor_dostoevsky-pushkin.html.

230 Fyodor Dostoyevsky, *A Writer's Diary*, Evanston, IL: North Western University Press, 2009.

231 George Mantzarides, *Orthodoxi Theologia kai Koinoniki Zoe* (in Greek, trans.: "Orthodox Theology and Social Life"), Salonika: Pournara, 1996, p. 181.

232 "The Orthodox Church has experienced and cultivated the idea of spiritual universality, which is a form of globalization, because she proclaims that all people from all nations and civilizations should be bound by ties of love, brotherhood, and cooperation. It is true that she calls for unity in one faith but does not view her love and interest as being conditional upon other people's acceptance of Orthodox Christianity as the true faith. Because she loves everyone, and fully experiences the unity of the humanity." Ecumenical Patriarch Bartholomew (1999), *Ethika Dilemmata tes Pagkosmiopoieseos* (in Greek, trans.: Ethical Dilemmas of Globalization), *Orthodoxia*, Issue A, p. 28.

233 See Rom 11:29.

The Orthodox Diaspora

234 " … For in one church there shall not be two bishops."

235 "We renounce, censure and condemn phyletism, that is racial discrimination, ethnic feuds, hatreds and dissensions within the Church of Christ, as contrary to the teaching of the Gospel and the holy canons of our blessed fathers which support the holy Church and the entire Christian world, embellish it and lead it to divine [piety]." Orthodox Wiki (May 15, 2019), *Phyletism*, retrieved on August 13, 2021, from: https://orthodoxwiki.org/Phyletism

236 See Matt 28:19.

237 "The concepts ecumenical (geographically) and catholic (universal) spiritually are conceptually identical, and relate to the fullness and universality of deliverance in Christ. The Church from the beginning acquired the character of a commonwealth. Not as a huge monolith of global proportions (like Papism), but as a galaxy of local churches, as constellations. Missionary activity works within this framework, as a constant call for 'unity in faith and communion of the Holy Spirit.' National consciousness did not act disruptively, because it is subjected to eternity and Faith. Hence there is no place for the development of racist consciousness. Throughout the history of the Church there is a golden thread connecting the Pentecost with the orthodox decision of the Synod in Constantinople of 1872 (condemnation of ethnophyletism in the life of the Church). Only after the frankification of the Christian West does missionary action go hand in hand with conquest, subjugation, colonization." George Metallenos (2008), "Orthodoxe Oikoumenikoteta kai Pagkosmiopoiese" (in Greek, trans.: Orthodox Universality and Globalization), *E Alle Opsis*, retrieved on August 15, 2021, from: https://alopsis.gr/ορθόδοξη-οικουμενικότητα-και-παγκοσ/.

238 Christos Giannaras, *The Inhumanity of Right* (N. Russell, Trans.), Cambridge: James Clarke Company, 2021.

239 Mark 9:35.

240 1 Cor 9:22.

241 " … if by the command of the Emperor a city be renewed, the order of ecclesiastical parishes shall follow the civil and public forms." Canon 17 of the Fourth Ecumenical Council.
"If any city be renewed by imperial authority, or shall have been renewed, let the order of things ecclesiastical follow the civil and public models." Canon 38 of Quintesext Ecumenical Council.

242 George Metallenos (2008), "Orthodoxe Oikoumenikoteta kai Pagkosmiopoiese" (in Greek, trans.: "Orthodox Universality and Globalization"), *E Alle Opsis*, retrieved on August 15, 2021, from: https://alopsis.gr/ορθόδοξη-οικουμενικότητα-και-παγκοσ/.

Orthodoxy and Inter-Orthodox, International Relations

243 "…if by the command of the Emperor a city be renewed, the order of ecclesiastical parishes shall follow the civil and public forms." Canon 17 of the Fourth Ecumenical Council.
"If any city be renewed by imperial authority, or shall have been renewed, let the order of things ecclesiastical follow the civil and public models." Canon 38 of Quintesext Ecumenical Council.

244 There is no set framework for the granting of autocephaly on the basis of Orthodox Canon Law. The discussions within the framework of preparation for the Panorthodox Synod in Crete brought about a preliminary agreement that for the granting of autocephaly there must be a unanimous agreement of all local Churches, but this preliminary agreement was not ratified. See Communique of Inter-Orthodox Preparatory Commission of 1993 available in Greek at: http://apostoliki-diakonia.gr/gr_main/dialogos/dialogos.asp?content=content&main=1993_pros_1.1.htm

245 "For the kingdom of God is not in word but in power. What do you want? Shall I come to you with a rod, or in love and a spirit of gentleness?" 1 Cor. 4:19–21.

246 As the Patriarchate of Constantinople has not fallen into heresy, there is no reason to lose or relinquish its privilege, honor, and duty of being first among equals, just because it is no longer the capital of the Roman (Byzantine) Empire. "For the gifts and the calling of God are irrevocable." Rom 11:29.

247 Below Constantinople, Alexandria, Antioch, and Jerusalem.

248 Although there is rarely any direct attempt by Russian ecclesiastical or political figures to question the primacy of the Ecumenical Patriarch, there is nonetheless clearly a general deliberate avoidance of the use of the term "Ecumenical" when referring to the Ecumenical Patriarch, preferring instead the term "Patriarch of Constantinople" in an obvious attempt to diminish his status.

249 See Communique of Inter-Orthodox Preparatory Commission of 1993 available in Greek at: http://apostoliki-diakonia.gr/gr_main/dialogos/dialogos.asp?content=content&main=1993_pros_1.1.htm

250 Demetrios Nikolakakis. *To Avtokephalon kai to Avtonomo sten poreia pros ten Agia kai Megale Synodo tes Orthodoxou Ekklesias* (not dated) (in Greek, trans.: "Autocephaly and Autonomy in preparation for the Holy and Great Synod of the Orthodox Church"), retrieved on August 17, 2021 from: http://www.ecclesia.gr/greek/press/theologia/material/2015_4_15_NIKOLAKAKIS.pdf

251 For more information as to the arguments expressed by both sides and the general climate of the discussions, see Ierotheos Vlachos (Metropolitan of Nafpaktos) (October 2008), *E Syzetese gia ten anakerykse Avtokephalias se mia Ekklesia* (in Greek, trans.: The Debate over the Declaration of Autocephaly in a Church), retrieved on August 17, 2021 from: http://athonikoipateres.gr/?p=47693.

252 In this way qualifying the rule of Canon 17 of the Fourth Ecumenical Council and Canon 38 of the Quinisext Ecumenical Council:
"…if by the command of the Emperor a city be renewed, the order of ecclesiastical parishes shall follow the civil and public forms." Canon 17 of the Fourth Ecumenical Council.
"If any city be renewed by imperial authority, or shall have been renewed, let the order of things ecclesiastical follow the civil and public models." Canon 38 of Quintesext Ecumenical Council.

253 Perhaps a gratitude similar to that which Paul encourages non-Judaic Christians to express toward Judaic Christians for the spiritual gifts received by the former from the latter: Rom 15:27.

254 Sarantis Michalopoulos (May 26, 2022), "Greece Sends More Weapons to Ukraine, Angering the Opposition," *Euractiv*, retrieved on September 7, 2022, from: https://www.euractiv.com/section/politics/short_news/greece-sends-more-weapons-to-ukraine-angering-the-opposition/

255 A step in the right direction is the fact that since September 2017 the Greek language is being optionally taught in schools throughout the Russian Federation. See Spiros Sideris (November 24, 2016), "Greek as an Optional Language in Russian Schools," *Independent Balkans News Agency*, retrieved on August 17, 2021, from: https://balkaneu.com/greek-optional-language-russian-schools/

Conclusions—Proposals

256 Eusebius, *The History of the Church from Christ to Constantine*, trans. G.A. Williamson (Baltimore: Penguin Books, 1965), p. 383.

257 Mark 2:27–28.

258   2 Cor 10:5.

259   Matt 4:19.

260   Matt 20:26.

Appendix

261   Richard Partington (April 19, 2022), "Russia 'Preparing Legal Action' to Unfreeze $600bn Foreign Currency Reserves," *The Guardian*, retrieved on September 1, 2022, from: https://www.theguardian.com/business/2022/apr/19/russia-preparing-legal-action-to-unfreeze-600bn-foreign-currency-reserves

262   Oliver Gordon (March 9, 2022), "What Will Be the Impact of Western Sanctions on Russia?" *Energy Monitor*, retrieved on September 2, 2022, from: https://www.energymonitor.ai/special-focus/ukraine-crisis/what-will-be-the-impact-of-western-sanctions-on-russia

263   Mark F. Cancian (May 23, 2022), "What Does $40 Billion in Aid to Ukraine Buy?" *Center for Strategic and International Studies*, retrieved on September 2, 2022, from: https://www.csis.org/analysis/what-does-40-billion-aid-ukraine-buy

264   Forum on the arms Trade, *Arms Transfers to Ukraine*, retrieved on September 2, 2022, from: https://www.forumarmstrade.org/ukrainearms.html

265   Anastasios, Archbishop of Tirana, *Eos Eschatou tes ges* (in Greek, trans.: To the Ends of the Earth), Athens: Apostoliki Diakonia, 2018.

266   The Conversation (March 17, 2022), "The History and Evolution of Ukrainian National Identity—Podcast" (Interview with Dominique Arel), retrieved on September 10, 2022, from: https://theconversation.com/the-history-and-evolution-of-ukrainian-national-identity-podcast-179279

267   The Conversation, *supra*.

268   Serhii M. Plokhy (1995), "The History of a 'Non-Historical' Nation: Notes on the Nature and Current Problems of Ukrainian Historiography," *Slavic Review*, vol. 54, no. 3, pp. 709–16, retrieved on September 9, 2022, from: https://doi.org/10.2307/2501745.

269   Antony C. Sutton, *Wall Street and the Bolshevik Revolution*, New Rochelle, NY: Arlington House, 1974.

270   Vladimir Putin (February 21, 2022), "Putin Says Modern Ukraine Was Created by Communist Russia," *YouTube*, retrieved on September 2, 2022, from: https://www.youtube.com/watch?v=81QS5sf8p5Y

271 Michael Pap (1952), "Soviet Difficulties in the Ukraine," *The Review of Politics*, vol. 14, no. 2, pp. 204–32, retrieved from: http://www.jstor.org/stable/1404967

272 Vladimir Putin (February 21, 2022), "Putin Says Modern Ukraine Was Created by Communist Russia," *YouTube*, retrieved on September 2, 2022, from: https://www.youtube.com/watch?v=81QS5sf8p5Y

273 John Armstrong, "Collaborationism in World War II: The Integral Nationalist Variant in Eastern Europe," *The Journal of Modern History*, vol. 40, no. 3 (September 1968), p. 409.
Jürgen Matthäus (April 18, 2013). *Jewish Responses to Persecution: 1941–1942.* Lanham, Maryland (USA): AltaMira Press. p. 524. ISBN 978-0759122598.

274 Christian Gerlach, "Kalkulierte Morde," Hamburg: Hamburger Edition, 1999.

275 Korrespondent.net (January 12, 2011), "Пресс-служба Януковича: Указ о присвоении Бандере звания Героя Украины отменен," retrieved on August 4, 2022, from: https://korrespondent.net/ukraine/politics/1164892-press-sluzhba-yanukovicha-ukaz-o-prisvoenii-bandere-zvaniya-geroya-ukrainy-otmenen

276 Massimo Introvigne (April 20, 2022), "Nazism in Ukraine—Separating Facts from Fiction," *Bitter Winter*, retrieved on August 4, 2022, from: https://bitterwinter.org/nazism-in-ukraine-separating-facts-from-fiction/

277 Tom Parfitt (August 11, 2014), "Ukraine Crisis: The Neo-Nazi Brigade Fighting Pro-Russian Separatists," *The Daily Telegraph*, retrieved on August 4, 2022, from: https://web.archive.org/web/20180705220331/https://www.telegraph.co.uk/news/worldnews/europe/ukraine/11025137/Ukraine-crisis-the-neo-Nazi-brigade-fighting-pro-Russian-separatists.html

278 Ali Tuygan (January 3, 2022), "Russia Proposes a New Security Architecture in Europe and Beyond," *The Guardian*, retrieved on August 4, 2022, from: https://edam.org.tr/en/russia-proposes-a-new-security-architecture-in-europe-and-beyond/?utm_source=rss&utm_medium=rss&utm_campaign=russia-proposes-a-new-security-architecture-in-europe-and-beyond

279 Mikhail Sergeevich Gorbachev, *Perestroika—New Thinking for Our Country and the World*, New York: Harper and Row, 1988.

280 Upravlenie delami presidenta Rossiskoi Federatsii (2022), *The Belavezha Accords Signed*, Boris Yeltsin Presidential Library, retrieved on September 6, 2022, from: https://www.prlib.ru/en/history/619792

281 Britannica (not dated), *People of Ukraine—Ethnic Composition (1991)*, retrieved on September 6, 2022, from: https://www.britannica.com/place/Ukraine/People

282 Britannica, *supra*.

283 Samuel Huntington, *The Clash of Civilizations and the Remaking of World Order*, New York: Simon & Schuster, 1996.

284 NATO (July 6, 2022), *Enlargement and Article 10*, retrieved on September 6, 2022, from: https://www.nato.int/cps/en/natolive/topics_49212.htm

285 Stathis N. Kalyvas and Nicholas Sambanis (2005), "Bosnia's Civil War," *Understanding Civil War*, p. 191, retrieved on September 9, 2022, from: https://stathiskalyvas.files.wordpress.com/2016/01/bosnia_000.pdf

286 John Catalinotto and Sara Flounders, *Hidden Agenda: US/NATO Takeover of Yugoslavia*, New York, NY: International Action Center, 2002.

287 Shireen M. Mazari, "NATO, Afghanistan and the Region," *Policy Perspectives*, vol. 5, no. 3 (2008), pp. 31–6, retrieved on May 7, 2022, from: http://www.jstor.org/stable/42909212.

288 John Pilger (September 22, 2003), "John Pilger Reveals That WMDs Were just a Pretext for Planned War on Iraq," *Mirror.co.uk*, retrieved on September 7, 2022, from: https://www.thedossier.info/articles/mirror_the-big-lie.pdf

289 C.R. Patrick Terry, "The Libya Intervention (2011): Neither Lawful, nor Successful," *The Comparative and International Law Journal of Southern Africa*, vol. 48, no. 2 (2015): 162–82, retrieved on September 8, 2022, from: http://www.jstor.org/stable/24585876.

290 Mark Mazzetti, Adam Goldman and Michael S. Schmidt (August 2,2017), "Behind the Sudden Death of a $1 Billion Secret C.I.A. War in Syria," *New York Times*, retrieved on September 9, 2022, from: https://www.nytimes.com/2017/08/02/world/middleeast/cia-syria-rebel-arm-train-trump.html

291 Kit Klarenberg (July 6, 2022), "Anatomy of a Coup: How CIA Front Laid Foundations for Ukraine War," *MRonline*, retrieved on September 7, 2022 from: https://mronline.org/2022/07/06/anatomy-of-a-coup/

292 Simon Pirani (January 20, 2019), "The Russian-Ukrainian Gas Conflict," *Russian Analytical Digest 53*, retrieved on September 11, 2022 from: https://web.archive.org/web/20160519104145/http://www.css.ethz.ch/content/dam/ethz/special-interest/gess/cis/center-for-securities-studies/pdfs/RAD-53.pdf

293 Szymon Kardaś, Agata Łoskot-Strachota and Konrad Popławski (September 9, 2015), "Gas Business as Usual? The New Agreements between Gazprom and EU Energy Companies," *Centre for Eastern Studies*, retrieved on September 11, 2022, from: https://www.osw.waw.pl/en/publikacje/analyses/2015-09-09/gas-business-usual-new-agreements-between-gazprom-and-eu-energy

294 Madeline Chambers and Sarah Marsh (February 22, 2022), "Germany Freezes Nord Stream 2 Gas Project as Ukraine Crisis Deepens," *Reuters*, retrieved on September 7, 2022, from: https://www.reuters.com/business/energy/germanys-scholz-halts-nord-stream-2-certification-2022-02-22/

295 Congressional Research Service (March 10, 2022), "Russia's Nord Stream 2 Natural Gas Pipeline to Germany Halted," retrieved on September 8, 2022, from: https://crsreports.congress.gov/product/pdf/IF/IF11138

296 Ted Galen Carpenter (August 6, 2017), "America's Ukraine Hypocrisy," *CATO Institute,* retrieved on September 7, 2022 from: https://www.cato.org/commentary/americas-ukraine-hypocrisy

297 Ian Traynor, (November 22, 2013), "Russia 'Blackmailed Ukraine to Ditch EU Pact," retrieved on September 7, 2022 from: https://www.theguardian.com/world/2013/nov/22/russia-ukraine-eu-pact-lithuania

298 Kit Klarenberg (July 6, 2022), "Anatomy of a Coup: How CIA Front Laid Foundations for Ukraine War," *MRonline*, retrieved on September 7, 2022, from: https://mronline.org/2022/07/06/anatomy-of-a-coup/

299 *BBC News.* "Ukraine Crisis: Leaders Agree Peace Roadmap" (February 12, 2015). Retrieved on September 7, 2022, from: https://www.bbc.com/news/world-europe-31435812

300 Al Jazeera (February 9, 2022), "*Ukraine-Russia Crisis: What Is the Minsk Agreement?*" *Al Jazeera*, retrieved on September 7, 2022, from: https://www.aljazeera.com/news/2022/2/9/what-is-the-minsk-agreement-and-why-is-it-relevant-now

301 Office of the United Nations Commissioner for Human Rights (not dated), *Report on the Human Rights Situation in Ukraine 1 December 2014 to 15 February 2015*, retrieved on September 8, 2022, from: https://www.ohchr.org/sites/default/files/Documents/Countries/UA/9thOHCHRreportUkraine.pdf

302 Office of the United Nations Commissioner for Human Rights, *supra.*

303 Tass (May 13, 2021), *"About 14,000 People Killed during Conflict in Donbass, Top Ukrainian Diplomat Says,"* retrieved on September 8, 2022, from: https://tass.com/world/1289095?utm_source=google. com&utm_medium=organic&utm_campaign=google.com&utm_ referrer=google.com

304 Office of the United Nations Commissioner for Human Rights (not dated), *Report on the Human Rights Situation in Ukraine 1 December 2014 to 15 February 2015*, retrieved on September 8, 2022, from: https://www.ohchr.org/sites/default/files/Documents/Countries/ UA/9thOHCHRreportUkraine.pdf

305 Ali Tuygan (January 3, 2022), "Russia Proposes a New Security Architecture in Europe and Beyond," *The Guardian*, retrieved on September 8, 2022, from: https://edam.org.tr/en/russia-proposes- a-new-security-architecture-in-europe-and-beyond/?utm_ source=rss&utm_medium=rss&utm_campaign=russia-proposes-a- new-security-architecture-in-europe-and-beyond

306 Elena Teslova (February 1, 2022), "US, NATO Ignore Russia's Principal Security Concerns: Putin," *Anadolu Agency*, retrieved on September 8, 2022, from: https://www.aa.com.tr/en/americas/us-nato-ignore- russias-principal-security-concerns-putin/2491266

307 Alex Leff (February 19, 2022), "A Rebel in East Ukraine Accused Kyiv of Planning an Attack. The U.S. Says He's Lying," *NPR*, Retrieved on September 11, 2022, from: https://www.npr. org/2022/02/18/1081790784/ukraine-evacuation-russia-donetsk

308 Congressional Research Service (March 10, 2022), "Russia's Nord Stream 2 Natural Gas Pipeline to Germany Halted," retrieved on September 8, 2022, from: https://crsreports.congress.gov/product/ pdf/IF/IF11138

309 Michelle Nichols (August 3, 2022), "West Could Trigger Nuclear War over Ukraine, Russia Says at U.N." *Reuters*, retrieved on September 8, 2022 from: https://www.reuters.com/world/europe/west-could- trigger-nuclear-war-over-ukraine-russia-says-un-2022-08-02/

Bibliography

Aglietta, Michel. *A Theory of Capitalist Regulation*. New York: Verso Books, 2001.

Al Jazeera (February 9, 2022). *"Ukraine-Russia Crisis: What Is the Minsk Agreement?."* *Al Jazeera*. Retrieved from: https://www.aljazeera.com/news/2022/2/9/what-is-the-minsk-agreement-and-why-is-it-relevant-now.

Anastasios, Archbishop of Tirana (June 14, 2016). "Epivevlimeni i Agia kai Megali Sinodos" (in Greek, trans.: "It Is Imperative for the Holy and Great Synod to Be Held"). *Kathimerini*. Retrieved from: http://www.kathimerini.gr/863672/article/epikairothta/ellada/ar8ro-anastasioy-sthn-k-epivevlhmenh-h-agia-kai-megalh-synodos.

Armstrong, John (September 1968). "Collaborationism in World War II: The Integral Nationalist Variant in Eastern Europe." *The Journal of Modern History* vol. 40, no. 3.

Athanasios, Metropolitan of Limassol (April 8, 2014). "E therapia apo tin arrostia tou Farisaismou" (in Greek, trans.: "The Therapy for the Disease of Pharisaism)." *Vima Orthodoxias*. Retrieved from: https://www.vimaorthodoxias.gr/eipan/lemesou-athanasios-oi-thriskoi-anthropoi-einai-to-pio-epikindyno-eidos-mesa-stin-ekklisia/.

Athanasios, Metropolitan of Limassol. *Kardiakos Logos* (in Greek, trans.: Word of the Heart). Holy and Great Monastery of Vatopaidi, 2021.

Bartholomew, Ecumenical (1999). *Ethika Dilemmata tes Pagkosmiopoieseos* (in Greek, trans.: Ethical Dilemmas of Globalization). *Orthodoxia*, Issue A.

BBC News (February 12, 2015). "Ukraine Crisis: Leaders Agree Peace Roadmap." Retrieved from: https://www.bbc.com/news/world-europe-31435812.

Britannica (not dated). *People of Ukraine—Ethnic Composition (1991)*. Retrieved from: https://www.britannica.com/place/Ukraine/People.

Cancian, Mark F. (May 23, 2022). "What Does $40 Billion in Aid to Ukraine Buy?" *Center for Strategic and International Studies*. Retrieved from: https://www.csis.org/analysis/what-does-40-billion-aid-ukraine-buy.

Carpenter, T.G. (August 6, 2017). "America's Ukraine Hypocrisy." *CATO Institute*. Retrieved from: https://www.cato.org/commentary/americas-ukraine-hypocrisy.

Catalinotto, John and Flounders, Sara. *Hidden Agenda: US/NATO Takeover of Yugoslavia*. New York, NY: International Action Center, 2002.

Chambers, M. and Marsh, S. (February 22, 2022). "Germany Freezes Nord Stream 2 Gas Project as Ukraine Crisis Deepens." *Reuters*. Retrieved from: https://www.reuters.com/business/energy/germanys-scholz-halts-nord-stream-2-certification-2022-02-22/.

Chrysostom, John. *On the Priesthood, Ascetic Treatises, Select Homilies and Letters, in Nicene and Post-Nicene Fathers*, vol. IX, First Series, ed. Schaff, Philip. Peabody, MA: Hendrickson Publishers, 1994.

Congressional Research Service (March 10, 2022). "Russia's Nord Stream 2 Natural Gas Pipeline to Germany Halted." Retrieved from: https://crsreports.congress.gov/product/pdf/IF/IF11138.

Devlin, Patrick. *The Judge*. Oxford: Oxford University Press, 1979.

Diels/ Kranz. Fragmente der Vorsokratiker, vol. I, 148.

Dostoyevsky, Fyodor. *A Writer's Diary*. Evanston, IL: North Western University Press, 2009.

Dostoyevsky, Fyodor. *Celebration of Pushkin's Birth, June 8 1880*. Retrieved from: http://www.speeches-usa.com/Transcripts/feyodor_dostoevsky-pushkin.html.

Dostoyevsky, Fyodor. *The Brothers Karamazov* (Ch. 5 "The Grand Inquisitor") (C. Garnett, Trans.). Retrieved from: https://www.mtholyoke.edu/acad/intrel/pol116/grand.htm.

EAEU, Eurasian Economic Union official website. Retrieved from: http://www.eaeunion.org/?lang=en#about-info.

Economou, Christos (not dated). *E symvole ton Elleniston Christianon ste Diadose tou Evangeliou sta Ethne* (in Greek, trans. : The Contribution of the Hellenistic Christians to the Spread of Christianity to the Nations). Retrieved from: http://www.kostasbeys.gr/articles.php?s=3&mid=1096&mnu=1&id=23171.

Epiphanius. *Panarion 69,2*, PG 42, 2014 AB.

Eusebius. *The History of the Church from Christ to Constantine*, trans. G.A. Williamson (Baltimore: Penguin Books, 1965).

Forum on the arms Trade, *Arms Transfers to Ukraine*. Retrieved from: https://www.forumarmstrade.org/ukrainearms.html.

Fotiou, Stavros. *The Church in the Modern World*. Berkeley: Inter-Orthodox Press, 2004.

Gerlach, Christian. *"Kalkulierte Morde."* Hamburg: Hamburger Edition, 1999.

Glenn, Patrick. *Legal Traditions of the World*, 4th edn. Oxford (England): Oxford University Press, 2010.

Goodrick-Clarke, Nicholas. *The Occult Roots of Nazism*. New York, NY: New York University Press.

Gorbachev, Mikhail Sergeevich. *Perestroika – New Thinking for Our Country and the World*. New York: Harper and Row, 1988.

Gordon, Oliver (March 9, 2022). "What Will Be the Impact of Western Sanctions on Russia?." *Energy Monitor*. Retrieved from: https://www.energymonitor.ai/special-focus/ukraine-crisis/what-will-be-the-impact-of-western-sanctions-on-russia.

Gvosdev, K. Nicholas. *Emperors and Elections, Reconciling the Orthodox Tradition with Modern Politics*. New York: Troitsa Books, 2000.

Havel, Vaclav. "The Power of the Powerless" (October 1978). *International Journal of Politics* (1979) pdf in website "ICNC, International Center on Nonviolent Conflict." Retrieved from: https://www.nonviolent-conflict.org/resource/the-power-of-the-powerless/.

Huntington, Samuel. *The Clash of Civilizations and the Remaking of World Order*. New York: Simon & Schuster, 1996.

Ignatius, Epistle to the Smyrnaeans. *New Advent*. Retrieved from: https://www.newadvent.org/fathers/0109.htm.

Introvigne, Massimo (April 20, 2022). "Nazism in Ukraine—Separating Facts from Fiction." *Bitter Winter*. Retrieved from: https://bitterwinter.org/nazism-in-ukraine-separating-facts-from-fiction/.

Isaac of Nineveh. *The Ascetical Homilies*. Holy Transfiguration Monastery, 2011.

Jehovah's Witnesses (not dated). *Why Don't Jehovah's Witnesses Go to War?* Retrieved from: https://www.jw.org/en/jehovahs-witnesses/faq/why-dont-jw-go-to-war/.

Kalyvas, Stathis N. and Sambanis, Nicholas. "Bosnia's Civil War." *Understanding Civil War* (2005): 191. Retrieved from: https://stathiskalyvas.files.wordpress.com/2016/01/bosnia_000.pdf.

Kardaś, Szymon, Agata, Łoskot-Strachota and Konrad, Popławski (September 9, 2015). "Gas Business as Usual? The New Agreements between Gazprom and EU Energy Companies." *Centre for Eastern Studies*. Retrieved from: https://www.osw.waw.pl/en/publikacje/analyses/2015-09-09/gas-business-usual-new-agreements-between-gazprom-and-eu-energy.

Karmires, Ioannis. *Ta dogmatika kai Symvolika Mnemeia tes Orthodoxou Katholikes Ekklesias*, vol. II. Athens, 1953.

Kavasilas, Nikolaos. *Peri tes en Christo zoes* (in Greek, trans.: About Life in Christ). Idhiotike, 2012.

Keselopoulos, Anestis. *Protaseis Poimantikes Theologias* (in Greek, trans.: Proposals in Pastoral Theology). Salonika: Pournaras, 2003.

Khawar, Hasaan (September 7, 2021). What Can Civil Service Learn from Military? *The Express Tribune*. Retrieved from: https://tribune.com.pk/story/2318863/what-can-civil-service-learn-from-military.

Kitsikis, Demetris. *E trite ideologia kai e Ordodoxia* (in Greek, trans.: The Third Ideology and Orthodoxy). Athens: Estia, 1998.

Klarenberg, Kit (July 6, 2022). "Anatomy of a Coup: How CIA Front Laid Foundations for Ukraine War." *MRonline*. Retrieved from: https://mronline.org/2022/07/06/anatomy-of-a-coup/.

Konidaris, John. *Egheiridio Ekklesiastikou Dikaiou* (in Greek, trans.: Manual of Ecclesiastical Law). Athens: Sakkoula 2000.

Korrespondent.net (January 12, 2011). "Пресс-служба Януковича: Указ о присвоении Бандере звания Героя Украины отменен." Retrieved from: https://korrespondent.net/ukraine/politics/1164892-press-sluzhba-yanukovicha-ukaz-o-prisvoenii-bandere-zvaniya-geroya-ukrainy-otmenen.

Kuprjanowicz, Tomasz. "Tsar Nicholas II—Heroism and Martyrdom." *Elpis* 21 (2019): 21–5.

Leff, Alex (February 19, 2022). "A Rebel in East Ukraine Accused Kyiv of Planning an Attack. The U.S. Says He's Lying." *NPR*. Retrieved from: https://www.npr.org/2022/02/18/1081790784/ukraine-evacuation-russia-donetsk.

Lenin, Vladimir I. *PSS* (Polnoe sobranie sochinenii) vol. 12.

Mantzarides, George. *Orthodoxi Theologia kai Koinoniki Zoe* (in Greek, trans.: Orthodox Theology and Social Life). Salonika: Pournara, 1996.

Marx, Karl and Engels, Friedrich (1872). *The Manifesto of the Communist Party*, "Chapter IV. Position of the Communists in Relation to the Various Existing Opposition Parties." Retrieved from: https://www.marxists.org/archive/marx/works/1848/communist-manifesto/ch04.htm.

Matthäus, Jürgen (April 18, 2013). *Jewish Responses to Persecution: 1941–1942*. Lanham, MD: AltaMira Press, p. 524. ISBN 978-0759122598.

Mazari, Shireen M. "NATO, Afghanistan and the Region." *Policy Perspectives* 5, no. 3 (2008): 31–6. Retrieved from: http://www.jstor.org/stable/42909212.

Mazzetti, Mark, Goldman, Adam and Schmidt, Michael S. (August 2, 2017). "Behind the Sudden Death of a $1 Billion Secret C.I.A. War in Syria." *New York Times*. Retrieved from: https://www.nytimes.com/2017/08/02/world/middleeast/cia-syria-rebel-arm-train-trump.html.

Metallenos, George. *E Ekklesia mesa ston kosmo* (in Greek, trans.: The Church in the World). Athens, Greece: Apostolike Diakonia tes Ekklesias tes Ellados, 1988.

Metallenos, George. *Ekklesia kai Politeia sten Orthodoxe Paradose* (in Greek, trans.: Church and State in the Orthodox Tradition). Athens: Armos, 2000.

Metallenos, George (2006). "Orthodoxia kai Fanatismos" (in Greek, trans.: "Orthodoxy and Fanaticism)." *E Alle Opsis*. Retrieved from: https://alopsis.gr/%ce%b-f%cf%81%ce%b8%ce%bf%ce%b4%ce%bf%ce%be%ce%af%ce%b1-%ce%ba%ce%b1%ce%b9-%cf%86%ce%b1%ce%bd%ce%b1%cf%84%ce%b9%cf%83%ce%b-c%cf%8c%cf%82-%cf%80%cf%81%cf%89%cf%84%ce%bf%cf%80%cf%81%ce%b5%cf%83%ce%b2/.

Metallenos, George (2008). "Orthodoxe Oikoumenikoteta kai Pagkosmiopoiese" (in Greek, trans.: "Orthodox Universality and Globalization)." *E Alle Opsis.* Retrieved from: https://alopsis.gr/ορθόδοξη-οικουμενικότητα-και-παγκοσ/.

Michalopoulos, Stamatis (May 26, 2022). "Greece Sends More Weapons to Ukraine, Angering the Opposition." *Euractiv.* Retrieved from: https://www.euractiv.com/section/politics/short_news/greece-sends-more-weapons-to-ukraine-angering-the-opposition/.

National Geographic (not dated). "Nation." Retrieved from: https://education.nationalgeographic.org/resource/nation.

NATO (July 6, 2022). *Enlargement and Article 10.* Retrieved from: https://www.nato.int/cps/en/natolive/topics_49212.htm.

Nichols, Michelle (August 3, 2022). "West Could Trigger Nuclear War over Ukraine, Russia Says at U.N." *Reuters.* Retrieved from: https://www.reuters.com/world/europe/west-could-trigger-nuclear-war-over-ukraine-russia-says-un-2022-08-02/.

Nicolaides, Nikos. *Themata Paterikis Theologias* (in Greek, trans.: Questions of Patristic Theology). Salonika: Lydia, 2009.

Nikolakakis, Demetrios. *To Avtokephalon kai to Avtonomo stin poreia pros ten Agia kai Megale Synodo tes Orthodoxou Ekklesias* (not dated) (in Greek, trans.: Autocephaly and Autonomy in Preparation for the Holy and Great Synod of the Orthodox Church). Retrieved from: http://www.ecclesia.gr/greek/press/theologia/material/2015_4_15_NIKOLAKAKIS.pdf.

Nodl, Martin (2010). "Summary." In Horníčková, Kateřina and Šroněk, Michal (eds.). *Umění české reformace (1380–1620) [The Art of the Bohemian Reformation (1380–1620)].* Praha: Academia, pp. 530–1.

Office of the United Nations Commissioner for Human Rights (not dated). *Report on the Human Rights Situation in Ukraine 1 December 2014 to 15 February 2015.* Retrieved from: https://www.ohchr.org/sites/default/files/Documents/Countries/UA/9thOHCHRreportUkraine.pdf.

Pap, Michael (1952). "Soviet Difficulties in the Ukraine." *The Review of Politics* 14, no. 2: 204–32. Retrieved from: http://www.jstor.org/stable/1404967.

Parfitt, Tom (August 11, 2014). "Ukraine Crisis: The Neo-Nazi Brigade Fighting Pro-Russian Separatists." *The Daily Telegraph.* Retrieved from: https://web.archive.org/web/20180705220331/https://www.telegraph.co.uk/news/worldnews/europe/ukraine/11025137/Ukraine-crisis-the-neo-Nazi-brigade-fighting-pro-Russian-separatists.html.

Partington, Richard (April 19, 2022). "Russia "Preparing Legal Action" to Unfreeze $600bn Foreign Currency Reserves." *The Guardian.*

Retrieved from: https://www.theguardian.com/business/2022/apr/19/russia-preparing-legal-action-to-unfreeze-600bn-foreign-currency-reserves.

Pilger, John (September 22, 2003). "The Big Lie—John Pilger Reveals That WMDs Were just a Pretext for Planned War on Iraq." *Mirror.co.uk*. Retrieved from: https://www.thedossier.info/articles/mirror_the-big-lie.pdf.

Pipes, Richard. *The Unknown Lenin*. New Haven and London: Yale University Press, 1999.

Pirani, Simon (January 20, 2019). "The Russian-Ukrainian Gas Conflict." *Russian Analytical Digest* 53. Retrieved from: https://web.archive.org/web/20160519104145/http://www.css.ethz.ch/content/dam/ethz/special-interest/gess/cis/center-for-securities-studies/pdfs/RAD-53.pdf.

Plokhy, Serhii. M. (1995). "The History of a 'Non-Historical' Nation: Notes on the Nature and Current Problems of Ukrainian Historiography." *Slavic Review* 54, no. 3: 709–16. Retrieved from: https://doi.org/10.2307/2501745.

Popovic, Justin. *Man and the God-Man*. Alhambra, CA: Sebastian Press Publishing House, 2008.

Putin, Vladimir (February 21, 2022). "Putin Says Modern Ukraine Was Created by Communist Russia." *YouTube*. Retrieved from: https://www.youtube.com/watch?v=81QS5sf8p5Y.

Re, Edward D. *The Roman Contribution to the Common Law*. 29 Fordham L. Rev. 447 (1961). Retrieved from: https://ir.lawnet.fordham.edu/flr/vol29/iss3/2.

Romanides, John. *Franks, Romans, Feudalism and Doctrine*. Brookline, MA.: Holy Cross Orthodox Press, 1981.

Romanides, John. *Dogmatike kai Symvolike Theologia tes Orthodoxou Katholikes Ekklesias* (in Greek, trans.: Dogmatic and Symbolic Theology of the Orthodox Catholic Church), vol. I, 4th edn. Salonika: Pournaras, 1999.

Romanides, John. *Romeosyne* (in Greek, trans.: Romanity). Thessaloniki: Pournaras, 2002.

Rozumna, Yulia and Soliman, Mina (2018). "The Consensus Patrum: What Is It?" *Orthodoxy in Dialogue*. Retrieved from: https://orthodoxyindialogue.com/2018/01/06/the-consensus-patrum-what-is-it-by-yulia-rozumna-and-mina-soliman/.

Runciman, Steven. *The Byzantine Theocracy*. Cambridge, UK: Cambridge University Press, 1977.

Sakharov, Sophrony. *St. Silouan the Athonite*. Crestwood, NY: St. Vladimir's Seminary Press, 1999.

Schmemann, Alexander. *The Mission of Orthodoxy*. Ben Lomond, CA: Conciliar Press, 1994.

Shakespeare, William (not dated). *Richard II.* Act 3, Scene 2, Verse 54–5. Retrieved from: https://www.sparknotes.com/nofear/shakespeare/richardii/page_118/.

Sideris, Spiros (November 24, 2016). "Greek as an Optional Language in Russian Schools." *Independent Balkans News Agency.* Retrieved from: https://balkaneu.com/greek-optional-language-russian-schools/.

Sutton Antony, C. *Wall Street and the Bolshevik Revolution.* New Rochelle, NY: Arlington House, 1974.

Tass (May 13, 2021). *About 14,000 People Killed during Conflict in Donbass, Top Ukrainian Diplomat Says.* Retrieved from: https://tass.com/world/1289095?utm_source=google.com&utm_medium=organic&utm_campaign=google.com&utm_referrer=google.com.

Terry, Patrick C.R. "The Libya Intervention (2011): Neither Lawful, nor Successful." *The Comparative and International Law Journal of Southern Africa* 48, no. 2 (2015): 162–82. Retrieved from http://www.jstor.org/stable/24585876.

Teslova, Elena (February 1, 2022). "US, NATO Ignore Russia's Principal Security Concerns: Putin." *Anadolu Agency.* Retrieved from: https://www.aa.com.tr/en/americas/us-nato-ignore-russias-principal-security-concerns-putin/2491266.

The Conversation (March 17, 2022). "The History and Evolution of Ukrainian National Identity—Podcast" (interview with Dominique Arel). Retrieved from: https://theconversation.com/the-history-and-evolution-of-ukrainian-national-identity-podcast-179279.

Theodoropoulos, Panagiotis. "Did the Byzantines Call Themselves Byzantines? Elements of Eastern Roman Identity in the Imperial Discourse of the Seventh Century." *Byzantine and Modern Greek Studies* 45, no. 1 (2021): 25–41. Retrieved from: https://www.cambridge.org/core/journals/byzantine-and-modern-greek-studies/article/did-the-byzantines-call-themselves-byzantines-elements-of-eastern-roman-identity-in-the-imperial-discourse-of-the-seventh-century/65B-940757F334DC5D5F0E6B479045BDD.

Tuygan, Ali (January 3, 2022). "Russia Proposes a New Security Architecture in Europe and Beyond." *The Guardian.* Retrieved from: https://edam.org.tr/en/russia-proposes-a-new-security-architecture-in-europe-and-beyond/?utm_source=rss&utm_medium=rss&utm_campaign=russia-proposes-a-new-security-architecture-in-europe-and-beyond.

Upravlenie delami presidenta Rossiskoi Federatsii (2022). *The Belavezha Accords Signed.* Boris Yeltsin Presidential Library. Retrieved from: https://www.prlib.ru/en/history/619792.

Vlachos, Ierotheos (Metropolitan of Nafpaktos). *The Person in the Orthodox Tradition*. Levadia, Greece: Birth of the Theotokos Monastery, 1999.

Vlachos, Ierotheos (Metropolitan of Nafpaktos) (October 2008). *E Syzetese gia ten anakerykse Avtokephalias se mia Ekklesia* (in Greek, trans.: The Debate over the Declaration of Autocephaly in a Church). Retrieved from: http://athonikoipateres.gr/?p=47693.

Wolff, Richard. *Democracy at Work: A Cure for Capitalism*. Chicago: Haymarket Books, 2012.

Yannaras, Christos. *Orthodoxia kai Dyse ste neotere Ellada* (in Greek, trans.: Orthodoxy and West in Modern Greece). Athens: Domos, 2006.

Yannaras, Christos. *Person and Eros*. Holy Cross Orthodox Press, 2008.

Yannaras, Christos. *E Eleftheria tou Ethous* (in Greek, trans.: The Freedom of Morals). Athens, Greece: Ikaros, 2011.

Yannaras, Christos. *The Inhumanity of Right* (N. Russell, Trans.). Cambridge: James Clarke Company, 2021.

Yanov, Alexander. *The Russian Challenge and the Year 2000*. New Jersey: Wiley–Blackwell 1987.

Zizioulas, John D. *Eucharist, Bishop, Church: The Unity of the Church in the Divine Eucharist and the Bishop during the First Three Centuries*. Brookline, MA: Holy Cross Orthodox Press, 2007.

Scripture Index

Index

HOLY TRINITY
PUBLICATIONS
Jordanville, New York

PSJP PRINTSHOP OF
SAINT JOB OF POCHAEV

HTSP HOLY TRINITY
SEMINARY PRESS

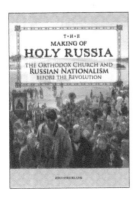

The Making of Holy Russia

The Orthodox Church and Russian Nationalism before the Revolution

By John Strickland

A critical study of the interaction between the Russian Church and society in the late nineteenth and early twentieth century. This work introduces the reader to a wide range of "conservative" opinions that strove for spiritual renewal and the spread of the Gospel. Illuminates current issues of Church-state relations and national identity in Eastern Europe.

ISBN: 9781942699279

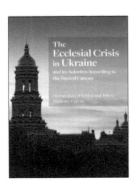

The Ecclesial Crisis in Ukraine

and its Solution According to the Sacred Canons

By Metropolitan of Kykkos and Tylliria, Nikiforos

"...a thoughtful and objective treatise for understanding the ecclesiastical crisis that has been created by the Ecumenical Patriarchate's granting autocephaly to schismatic groups in Ukraine."

+TIMOTHEOS, Metropolitan of Bostra

ISBN: 9781942699415

Foundations of Russian Culture

By Alexander Schmemann

At a time when tensions between Russia and "the West" are increasing, this book is very timely, even though, its contents were first broadcast over fifty years ago. It offers a history of Russian culture and its particular trends and tendencies, which are shown to be frequently contradictory and even mutually exclusive. Schmemann argues for the supremacy of culture over political life in determining questions such as the apparent lack of political freedoms, law and order and civil rights in a Russian context.

ISBN: 9781942699507